SPIT OUT THE APPLE!

How to Embrace God's love...

By rejecting the gift He never gave you

By Ken Franklin

To Terri, my soulmate;
To Debi, my Godgift;
To Christ, my redeemer;
To God, who Loves.

I will eternally Love You back.

Table of Contents

Introduction.. 1
   What do You Want From This Book?..... 3
   Where I'm Coming From 9
   The Driving Gasp 15
The Apple 21
   Three Gifts 23
   Why Do Things Go Wrong?.................. 31
Getting to "I AM" 39
   The Case for God 41
   God is Not a Job Applicant 53
   Command and Control.......................... 63
   Religion vs. Spirituality vs. Faith 71
Verbs versus Nouns 77
   The Danger of the Noun....................... 79
   Commit to Loving Back........................ 91
   The Practice Effect 111
The Eternal Opponent............................... 123
   Loving in Noise and Traffic 125
   Punching Jesus in the Face 137
   The Enemy's Quiver of Weapons........ 139
   Cans and Can'ts 163
Living Without the Apple 185
   The Value of a Covenant Partner 187
   The Value of Small Groups 195
   Resilience vs. Fearfulness..................... 201
   The Ite People....................................... 213
   We are All Headed to Golgotha 223
   Scorecards are Apple-flavored 229
Here! Have a Present! I Love You!.............. 241

Introduction

Ken Franklin

What do you want from this book?

You picked up this book for a reason. Ask yourself what that is.

Are you looking for something to back up your point of view?

Are you looking to quiet a pain in your life?

Are you looking to improve yourself?

Are you looking to be entertained?

Whatever you want, I would ask that you take one step back, and ask: *Why do you want?*

We human beings seem to be ruled by our wants, and we try to wrestle the world to the ground so that we get those wants met. Then, we often find that it's not *really* what we wanted, or we can't stop wanting more of it, or we fail to get that want filled… in short, wanting can waste your life.

So, let's figure out – why do we want?

This book is not a course. It's a story.

I am not a pastor. I am not, strictly speaking, a teacher, though my career has included a great deal of teaching. I am, however, a pretty good storyteller. I hope to help you explore things, and maybe lead you to some helpful conclusions, mainly through the use of stories.

Why stories work better

We have all sat through classroom lectures. We can remember teachers or professors who droned on and on from prepared notes on a subject they were trying to insert into your brain in a way that led to: "Oh wait – why am I drooling on my desk and how long have I been asleep?"

Many of us also have favorite teachers. Teachers who engaged us; who challenged us; who made us chase after learning. What characteristics do such teachers share? Recent research has shown that they all use stories to teach. Memorization of lists of facts gives us good memories, but does not connect those facts to realities. Stories, on the other hand, provide us with experiences, and experiences are things we can integrate into our lives.

Trade guilds build skilled workers by showing people problems in real life, watching how others solve them, and then learning how to become the problem-solver. Medical school is little different. (I'm a retired family physician, but we'll get to that later; this isn't about me.) Medical students, interns, residents, and specialty fellows learn by listening to patients' stories, watching how senior physicians diagnose and solve their problems, and then learning how to become the problem-solver. And tying book lists of diagnoses into medical stories cements knowledge forever in physician's brains.

The value of parables

Why did Jesus tell stories? Most of the teaching during His adult ministry came in the form of stories called parables. One reason is to fulfill prophecy, as He explained:

> His disciples came and asked him, "Why do you use parables when you talk to the people?"
>
> He replied, "You are permitted to understand the secrets of the Kingdom of Heaven, but others are not. To those who listen to my teaching, more understanding will be given, and they will have an abundance of knowledge. But for those who are not listening, even what little understanding they have will be taken away from them. That is why I use these parables, For they look, but they don't really see. They hear, but they don't really listen or understand.
>
> "This fulfills the prophecy of Isaiah that says, 'When you hear what I say, you will not

understand. When you see what I do, you will not comprehend. For the hearts of these people are hardened, and their ears cannot hear, and they have closed their eyes – so their eyes cannot see, and their ears cannot hear, and their hearts cannot understand, and they cannot turn to me and let me heal them.'

"But blessed are your eyes, because they see; and your ears, because they hear." –Matthew 13:10–16 (NLT)

In using parables, Christ was also trying to relate revolutionary ideas to the culture His audience was living in; simply stating His point would come across as proposing an opinion rather than speaking with authority. Christ knew that some people were not ready for His teachings, and told His disciples as much in this passage. Finally, in the tense atmosphere of the Pharisee's governance under Roman occupation, Christ had to avoid direct statements that would become evidence for a charge of treason or blasphemy. (Obviously, this avoidance didn't prevent accusation by the religious leaders in power, though it did prevent them from being able to convict him without fabricating evidence.)

Parables are stories. So, when I build stories for you, I am trying to imitate Christ. But since there are no Romans trying to execute me, and since I'm not fulfilling ancient prophecy, I hope that you'll get the point of these stories.

So – here's the story.

Here's what I want:

I hope to love you by showing, to my way of thinking, the single biggest thing keeping us separate from a relationship with God.

In case you're having trouble with God as a concept, I hope to introduce you to Him.

And finally, I hope to show you several ways that you can experience the peace and joy that comes from a relationship with Him.

Why do I want that?

Why do I want?

I want because I feel so totally loved. And I see so many around me who do not.

I'm willing to bet you're one of those people.

I want to be the deliveryman of the answer to your want, in an act of loving Christ back.

Even though doing that one billion times would not begin to repay His gift to me – loving Christ back will remain the *want* that drives my life. For Eternity.

So here's a present for you. Here's your delivery. I made this for you. I hope it fulfills your want. And your why.

Where I'm Coming From

If you want to get right to the book, I suggest you skip the next two chapters and start reading at "Three Gifts" on page 23. But if, for any reason, you want to get to know me before you start trusting me, let me tell you my story.

• • •

I was baptized as an infant, and raised a Christian by my loving paternal grandma Emma. Emma was a disciple and saint all of her life. When my parents messily divorced after 9 years, her love and the support of my local church kept me sane.

Shortly after the divorce, my father transitioned from the Army National Guard to Active Duty. Because of frequent military moves, regular church attendance was hard to come by. (Surviving as the family of a single father of two in the 1960s and 1970s was difficult enough.) I retained my faith, but biblical teaching suffered, and by the time I reached college, I thought George Burns in the comedy film "Oh, God" was an accurate representation of the God of Abraham, Moses, David, and Jesus Christ.

I met and married my soulmate, Terri Tamlyn, in 1977, near the end of college and ROTC training. I started my military career by entering medical school at the Uniformed Services University of the Health Sciences. Through medical school and my family medicine residency, Terri and I shared a strong belief in Christ, and tried living a Christian life. However, I fell into the trap of believing that my salvation was based solely on my own talents and my own efforts. I was living "God Helps Those Who Help Themselves" (a great sentiment by Ben Franklin, but nowhere near Biblical).

In 1984, I was humbled by receiving my 10th-choice assignment after residency. I drove there on a house-hunting trip, sullen and bitter, with a very pregnant Terri beside me. After the first day of sizing up a small town in the middle of nowhere, we were crying in each other's arms when we simultaneously heard the Spirit: "God has us there for a reason." Keep in mind: we had been to church maybe 5 times in the past 3 years. We prayed and submitted our will to God, and in the next 72 hours, the house of our dreams went on the market, Terri had a solid job lead, and my department head told me to design my dream job, and he'd make it happen.

We resumed regular church attendance shortly afterwards.

For the rest of my 25 years in the Army, I worked hard to listen to God's leading in all areas of my life. He blessed me with two wonderful sons, and Terri and I enjoyed fulfilling careers. I discovered that my faith was at odds with the politics required at senior levels of Army leadership, and chose to return to full-time clinical practice. I retired in 2002. We were led to a wonderful privately-owned small group practice in Vicksburg, Michigan, a 3000-person suburb of Kalamazoo.

I believed that Terri and I had decades to claim all of the delayed gratification we had stored up so far in our lives.

Then, in 2006, at age 49, Terri developed a near-fatal bowel obstruction from stage 4 colon cancer. She underwent emergency surgery and came home with a colostomy.

With the help of a wonderful healing and anointing service in our living room, God cleansed Terri of her initial disease. We lived her dreams until the cancer returned 3 years later, and in August of 2010 she beat that miserable disease by flying into Christ's arms.

The next years were difficult, and I am very open and honest when I tell people that without the prayer support of my sons and church family, I would have committed suicide. But God never left my side – and I never left His.

Terri had made it clear to me and to her female friends that she wanted me to remarry. I made some brief attempts at dating, and even signed up with an online matchmaking service. But above all, I listened to the guidance of Griefshare's excellent book, <u>Through a Season of Grief</u>: "If God has another partner for you, He will provide one. Don't rush it." So I accepted that I would likely be single for the rest of my days.

In 2012, I received an email inviting me to a "speed-dating" event. I was floored. That night, when I was kneeling in prayer, I asked: "God, is this from You? Do You have someone for me?" The answer was loud, audible and unmistakable: "YES!" So I went to the event, and though nothing came of it, I went back to the online dating service, and stated clearly that I was looking for a Christian woman who had lost her spouse to cancer.

That's how I met Debi Neddo. She matched number 1, even though she told me later that she had cancelled her account 3 days before I searched.

Debi had grown up in Kalamazoo, and had lived in Michigan most of her life. She had married a pastor and musician, Mike, and they had two sons very close in age to my sons. Then Mike had developed aggressive prostate cancer at age 50, which led to his passing in 2004. She had been fruitlessly looking for another mate, off and on, for 8 years. Her sons had encouraged her to "lighten up on the Christian stuff" in her dating profile, but she held firm. She told them, "I'll know he's the right one when his first email says, 'You're just the person I've been looking for'".

And that's how I introduced myself.

We met in October, dated for 2 months, and I realized she was the woman God had in mind for me. So I followed Billy Crystal's advice in the movie "When Harry Met Sally": when you find the person you want to spend the rest of your life with, you want the rest of your life to start as soon as possible! We were engaged near Christmas, and married in March of 2013.

This was not merely a marriage of hormones and desperation. We had some very frank talks before we became engaged. Each of us had already endured the worst pain and grief that anyone could experience, and we knew that someday, one of us would experience it again. We hoped it would be a long time from now, but there were no guarantees.

We made it clear to each other's families that we would completely honor the lifetime gifts of Mike and Terri. We also made it clear that this marriage would be led, daily and unreservedly, by God.

We have had six years together as I write this. I have retired from family medicine, and we have continued to laugh with joy at our life together. Debi is an extremely talented quilter, and enjoys camping and the water. I enjoy speaking as a lay servant, and have taken my love of tabletop games to new levels as a game designer. We sometimes refer to ourselves as "The Squire and the Squarer."

I am far more blessed than any human could earn. I have more blessings than any lottery winner in history. And my life is full of delight.

But life is not perfect: for instance, there was the problem of the Driving Gasp.

The Driving Gasp

Debi and I were married when I was 57. Of course, we were both in the second half of our youth, so we were pretty experienced at doing adult things. That means we each had a way of doing things that we had practiced for a long time.

That also meant that we had both driven a car. A lot. And we were both used to driving most of the time.

So while we were still dating, and I was driving us on a date, I first heard it.

The Gasp.

I jumped a bit. I looked around for what was wrong. I glanced over to see if Debi was in pain; she seemed all right. I asked her what was wrong. She said, "I saw that car approaching, and I was afraid you might have missed it."

I had seen the car, and had already taken it into account – but not precisely in the way she would have. So we drove on.

That trip, I heard the gasp two more times. Sometimes she would gasp just as I was starting to slow down, because she wasn't sure I was *going* to slow down. Sometimes she saw a lane closure, and didn't think I had seen it.

This continued for a few days. Then I said, "Honey, I know how to drive. I've been driving for decades. I promise I'll take good care of you. I won't get into an accident."

But the gasps continued. Even after we were married.

You see, I started to feel like she didn't trust me. And no matter how I tried to learn what things caused the gasps, and no matter how I tried to adjust my driving style to prevent the gasps – the gasps still came.

At the same time, Debi was getting more and more anxious, because she knew the gasps bothered me, but working to hold them in only made her more hyper-vigilant, and more anxious.

It got to the point that we developed a pattern: gasp from her; harrumph from me; tears from her; tears from me; pull over the car.

The problem got *really* pronounced after we decided to buy a 27-foot travel trailer and a pickup to tow it. The first time we practiced backing it up? Gasp city. And I got so frustrated that I actually *did* scratch the trailer with the back of the truck.

So, I had to ask myself: *why do I want?*

I knew *what* I wanted: I wanted to be seen as the perfect driver, caring for my wife. And I didn't want to feel like I was constantly being judged and found wanting. I didn't want to try my hardest – and still fail. I didn't want my wife to be afraid of me.

But WHY did I want?

Because I had been given love after I thought I would never love again. And I was terrified I would lose it.

And Debi was similarly terrified.

We discussed our fears, and started (as, thankfully, we always do) by reaffirming the covenant of our marriage. We will not let *anything*, said or unsaid, break the covenant of love that we made with God. Furthermore, I learned that Debi was always anxious on the road, because of a car accident that broke her wrist and caused her to miscarry a pregnancy in 1983, followed by another a rear-end surprise that endangered her son in 2001.

Armed with that information, I taught myself not to feel threatened by the Driving Gasp. I practiced saying "Thank You" or "I see it" when she pointed out a concern. Over a year or so, I now have complete peace with it; and over the same time, Debi has learned not to feel guilty when she does it.

Mind you, the Driving Gasp still happens occasionally. Last year, she gasped and immediately apologized. I said, "You don't need to apologize, darling. Your gasp is an expression of love and caring. It reminds me to drive in a way that gives you the most peace. I love you."

We drove on in silence for a couple of minutes. Then Debi said, "Ken, your approach to love and faith is nothing I have ever seen before. It's powerful and important. You should write a book about it."

That statement floored me, but since my Godly wife is pretty smart, I asked God about it. He agreed, as did my closest prayer partners and my pastor.

So now you're reading it. That's my story.

The reason I am able to achieve the peace that Debi noticed is that I have noticed a common thread in all my anxieties, fears, and frustrations. That common thread came from the Garden of Eden.

I'd like to tell you a story about that, too.

Discussion Questions

1. Do you have a pet peeve? Is there a behavior that "pushes your buttons?" How do you deal with it?

2. Do you have a way to defuse your anger when someone pushes your button? How effective is it?

3. Do you have a helpful Bible passage about reconciling disagreements? About dealing with annoying behavior from a friend or spouse?

The Apple

Ken Franklin

Three Gifts

The Bible, in Matthew 2:1–12, tells the story of the three Wise Men who followed a star to see the newborn king. (If you're already arguing in your head about whether they were magi, or kings, or wise men, or Zoroastrian astrologers, keep reading! I wrote this book for you.) They brought three precious commodities as gifts to the Christ-child: Gold, Frankincense, and Myrrh.

The Life Application New Testament Commentary[1] pointed out the significance of these three gifts, and their symbolism:

Gold represents wealth, power, and high status. It was a gift of riches. It was a gift for someone who held dominion over others; a gift for a king.

Frankincense is an aromatic gum resin. The word literally means high-quality incense. When burned, it gives off a very pleasant aroma. It was specified by God in the book of Leviticus as an ingredient in burnt offerings. It

---

[1] Page 14. Life Application New Testament Commentary by Bruce Barton et al, ©2001 by the Livingstone Corporation, published by Tyndale House Publishers, Inc.

was a gift of worship. It was a gift of honor; a gift for a deity.

Myrrh was a different aromatic gum resin. It had medicinal, antibiotic, and preservative properties. As such, it was commonly used to embalm the dead. It has a much more bitter aroma. Myrrh was a gift to acknowledge sacrifice. It was a gift of preservation; a gift for the dead.

These gifts, when sold, went a long way to paying for Joseph and Mary's living expenses, including the costs of fleeing to Egypt when King Herod ordered the wholesale slaughter of young boys. However, these gifts also represented all of the prophecy of the life of Christ. But I have noticed that they also connect to a much earlier place where three gifts were bestowed:

The Garden of Eden.

In the book of Genesis, there were also three gifts given to Adam and Eve (and thus to humanity). They were much more miraculous and exorbitant than the gifts of the Wise Men. And each of the gifts had a parallel significance.

Just as the Magi gave gold, God gave humans a gift for a king. God gave humans, and humans alone, free will and dominion. God gave Adam and Eve, and their offspring, the Godlike ability to make their own choices, and to hold the highest status of guides and stewards for the entire earth.

Just as the Magi gave Frankincense, God gave humans a gift for a deity. God gave humans love and life. God gave Adam and Eve, and their offspring, the ability to celebrate living without shame. Humanity was invited into a direct, personal relationship with God, with love, joy, and acceptance. God provided the ability, and the preference, to live face to face with each individual in one-on-one terms.

Now the third gift did not come from God. It came from the serpent.

> *The Lord God placed the man in the Carden of Eden to tend and watch over it. But the Lord God warned him, You may freely eat the fruit of every tree in the garden— except the tree of the knowledge of good and evil. If you eat its fruit, you are sure to die." –Genesis 2:15–17 (NLT)*

Please note that the God does NOT say, "if you eat of it I will kill you." God does NOT say, "If you eat of it I will stop loving you." God is not threatening like an abusive parent. He is warning like a loving parent, much like we would tell our children not to eat broken glass, play with razor blades, or dance on the freeway.

Back to Scripture:

Now the serpent was more crafty than any of the wild animals the Lord God had made. He said to the woman, "Did God really say, 'You must not eat from any tree in the garden'?"

The woman said to the serpent, "We may eat fruit from the trees in the garden, but God did say, 'You must not eat from the tree that is in the middle of the garden, and you must not touch it, or you will die.'"

"You will not certainly die," the serpent said to the woman, "For God knows that when you eat of it your eyes will be opened, and you will be like God, knowing good and evil."

When the woman saw that the fruit of the tree was good for food and pleasing to the eye, and also desirable for gaining wisdom, she took some and ate it. She also gave some to her husband, who was with her, and he ate it. – Genesis 3:1–6 (NLT)

Just as the Magi gave Myrrh, the third gift (a gift from the Serpent) was for Adam, Eve, and their offspring, a gift for the dying: the knowledge of Good and Evil. The ability to evaluate. The ability to classify. The ability to sort. The ability to judge.

The Apple.

Which of these three gifts do you find the most valuable?

Which of these three gifts would you want to return?

Which of those three gifts do you use the most?

When you examine yourself, do you use your free will to make choices to love and care for yourself? Do you use love and relationship to listen to God, and learn from his Word? Or do you dwell on your faults and past mistakes – worry about your future – nurture bitterness and despair?

When you examine others, do you look for ways to teach and uplift each other? Do you look for things to appreciate, to love, to celebrate? Do you look for the image of God present in every other human being? Or do you make snap judgments based on initial impressions and appearance, and jump at the chance to issue judgment on the value and rightness (or wrongness) of others?

Don't get me wrong; we are all fallible, fallen people. I fall into this trap myself, especially when I watch the news or read stories about politics. We cannot return the third gift on our own.

Rejoice and hear the Good News: God, as Christ, already accepted humiliation, torture, monumental pain, and death as payment in full for your failings! He loved you that much!

He chose death on a cross. He made the choice of a Benevolent King.

He loves everyone that much. He showed the Love of a perfect Deity.

He denounced condemnation through His death. He chose death over separation from you.

Which gifts does God want you to use? Which gift does God want you to put away?

God refuses to take away the first two gifts. That, in itself, is evidence of how amazing God is, and how deeply He loves you.

You, and you alone, have the ability to use your gifts of free will, dominion over your life, and the ability to love – to return the third gift.

To Spit Out the Apple.

To give up your private throne and love others as you are loved.

Think of all you could accomplish if you were freed of that poisonous task!

I have been repeating this request to friends and groups for many years. Unfortunately, most of the time I get responses like, "Nice thoughts. Well said. Thank you for that." When I ask why, the most common rebuttal is, "But there is so much wrong with the world!" As if being able to label all the wrong gives us power over the wrong.

Well, let's look at that for a bit.

Discussion Questions

1. What kinds of things cause you to end friendships?

2. Have you ever "blocked" or "unfriended" someone on social media? What caused it? Do you regret it?

3. Did you ever wish you were in charge of the world? If so, what would you change? What might go wrong with your idea?

Why Do Things Go Wrong?

Many, many books have been written on the subject of evil and suffering on the planet. I submit there is a very simple answer:

We have suffering in the world because we, as humanity, have chosen it, daily, for thousands of years. And God loves us too much to take back the gifts he gave us.

The original meaning of sin is "missing the mark." Let's be generous and assume each human being misses the mark only once a day. If you do some very rough calculus of the population of the earth over the past 6000 years, that means there has been a MINIMUM of 730 BILLION sins committed by humanity. Imagine if each sin was an arrow missing a target.

That's a pretty big heap of arrows.

In you imagine the hurt and damage lingering behind each of these sins, in terms of damage to the earth and each other, you can pretty much account for the majority of hardship on this planet.

True, humanity is not at fault for geology and weather. But we, as a species, have pointedly asked a deity that builds planets for a living to butt out of our world. And because He gave us free will, and dominion, He honored our request.

In order for God to prevent all suffering on this Earth, one of two things has to happen: either God takes back the gift of free will and uses us as slave-like puppets – or we all have to choose to re-enter relationship with Him of our own free will.

I hear you say, "That would never work." But how else would you account for the tens of thousands of personal miracles that have occurred in our history?

I already described personal examples of miracles in my life in the introduction. Let me tell you two others.

I already mentioned that my first wife, Terri, developed Stage 4 cancer in 2006 at age 49. She underwent emergency surgery to remove part of her colon (leaving her with a colostomy pouch), followed by 4 months of chemotherapy. After the colostomy was reversed, she was pronounced cancer-free. Of course, we remained vigilant, since microscopic colon cancer can spread undetected through the bloodstream.

Terri's cancer came back again June 3rd, 2009, four days before my second son, Jeremy, graduated high school.

We met with her oncologist on June 10th and planned her chemotherapy. Later that evening, we decided to take our minds off our pain by working in our garden. I was trying to get my little mini-tiller started for the first time that year. After about 20 minutes of false starts and sputters, I lost my temper, throwing the tiller 20 feet across the yard – followed by my shoes. I stood there in tears – at the end of my strength. Terri came up and hugged me – similarly empty.

It had been completely overcast all that day. But right there, Terri gasped and said, "Look!" The sun broke through the clouds, and a sunbeam 20 feet across hit us where we stood. The temperature went up 20 degrees in 5 seconds. And we felt loved, protected, and renewed.

Terri defeated cancer by flying into Christ's arms on August 3, 2010. It was by far the greatest pain I have ever, or will ever, endure. I still weep often about her absence, just as my wife Debi weeps over the loss of her beloved Mike.

But that leads me to my second example of a personal miracle:

I look a lot at sunrises and sunsets.

One of the things that Terri and I loved the most about our home in Vicksburg was the beautiful view of the eastern and western skies – and all the spectacular Michigan sunrises and sunsets that we could see. I have many of our photos of such times; they make me smile.

On May 19, 2011, as the sun started to go down, I noted rays of sunlight surrounding very long shadows of the house. I looked out the front door to see if there was a spectacular sunset; but nahhh. It had rained most of the day, and the clouds were all to the east. The western sky was clear.

Still, I thought of Terri, and I said aloud: "Oh, darling. I miss you so. I know you're happy; but do you look down on me? Can you see me? Do you spend any of your joyous time looking at me? I'd like to know." I wept for a bit, then returned to checking my email.

Two minutes later, our little dog Osgrr barked. Once. (That in itself was remarkable: Osgrr NEVER barks only once.) I looked up, through the east-facing window of my office. There, silhouetted against the retreating rain, was the brightest rainbow I've seen in my entire life. It arose from our hayfield, and made about a third of an arc before disappearing above; but at its center there were three clearly visible sets of the spectrum.

I watched it for a long time. I'd needed a hug like that from her for months. It felt so very, very good.

Now I am confident that at least one person reading this will dismiss it as a coincidence of the weather, the time of day, and my wishful thinking. They would argue, "The laws of physics don't leave room for such personal, individual miracles." Some would label me delusional.

However, that Sunday, my friend John, who lives about 3 miles to the northwest, happened to be out for a walk. He also saw the same rainbow; and he remarked feeling certain that it was coming from my backyard.

So go ahead and label me delusional if this causes you cognitive dissonance[2]. I won't change my mind. I choose to believe that I asked a question, and the Creator of the Universe let my true love answer it.

In addition to these two examples, I have witnessed several medical miracles in my career as a family physician:

---

[2] **cognitive dissonance** (noun) The state of having inconsistent thoughts, beliefs, or attitudes, especially as relating to behavioral decisions and attitude change. The term is often applied to situations where one's core belief is challenged by a statement or experience.

- The sudden appearance of masses on both ovaries in an elderly woman, with malignant appearance on a CT[3] scan, that were found to be completely benign during surgery;

- The discovery of a large complex malignant mass around the gall bladder in another elderly woman that had turned completely to benign scar tissue when removed 6 weeks later;

- A baby proven to have anencephaly (congenital absence of a head) in two second-trimester ultrasounds, but born completely normal; and

- A woman with crippling rheumatoid arthritis, whose fingers were bent sideways at a 30 degree angle. After 36 hours of fasting and nonstop prayer, her hands were completely healed.

There are many books full of examples of personal miracles, many more powerful than mine. I especially like the "It's a God Thing" series by Don Jacobson and K-LOVE[4], as well

---

[3] CT means Computed Tomography. It is a detailed cross-sectional look at our internal anatomy.
[4] By Donald C. Jacobson, Published by W Publishing, an imprint to Thomas Nelson.

as the excellent book "Finding God in the Waves" by Mike "Science Mike" McHargue.[5]

These are not always due to prayer. These miracles were often not earned. But miracles happen. And in my reading, they appear far more often to people who live in relationship with God.

Unconvinced? Maybe there is a different "why do I want" here. I see the question behind your question. You're not asking why God permits suffering. You're asking if suffering is evidence that God doesn't exist. You're not sure if Jesus and God are real. You're asking why you should believe all this Garden of Eden stuff.

That's a fair question. Let's stop for a chapter or two and ponder it.

Discussion Questions

1. Have you ever witnessed a miracle? How did you feel when it happened?

2. Do you have a question to ask God when you get to Heaven?

3. Is there something on Earth that makes you doubt God's existence? Is there something

---

[5] ©2016 by Mike McHargue, published by Convergent Books, an imprint of Crown Publishing Group, a division of Penguin Random House LLC.

on Earth that makes you doubt God's goodness?

Getting to "I AM"

Ken Franklin

The Case for God

Let me start here by pointing out: this chapter is going to refer you to several authors. They have studied, and written on, the evidence of a creator far deeper and far better than I can. However, in the interest in saving you money, and in the interest of getting back to the issue of Spitting Out the Apple, I want to summarize their work here.

The Big Bang

My first piece of evidence of a creator is the nature of our universe's existence. Stephen Hawking, in his astounding book "A Brief History of Time,"[6] makes a convincing case that the universe started from a singularity referred to as "The Big Bang". Throughout the book, Hawking states that his curiosity of this search stems partially from trying to determine the nature, and the existence, of God. After all, if the universe had no beginning or end (a theory known as the "Steady-State Theory"), then a creation could not have happened.

---

[6] ©1988, 1996, 2017 by Stephen Hawking. Published in the US by Bantam Books, an imprint of Random House, a division of Penguin Random House, LLC.

Hawking's book ends with convincing evidence that the Big Bang was indeed the origin of the universe. In fact, measurements taken since Hawking's book confirm that the universe is actually expanding at an accelerating speed. (At the time of this writing, nobody can agree why that is.)

However, in other writings, Professor Hawking ascribed a belief in something called "M-theory", an incomplete attempt to unify all the forces of nature into a single force in multiple dimensions. (M-theory was first proposed in 1995 by Edward Witten.) Hawking stated that the existence of M-theory made the existence of a creator not necessary to create the universe, and therefore accepted atheism as a belief.

My counterargument is that just because an alternative possibility exists, that does not disprove the universe as a creation of God. Further, Hawking's argument completely overlooks a huge piece of evidence that is a lot smaller than the universe: our genetic structure.

The DNA Question

All life on earth, from the simplest virus to human beings, uses DNA and RNA to encode the instructions for its construction and operation. Each of us contains, in every cell with a nucleus, the biochemical equivalent of a book with 2,900,000,000 letters in it – each letter being A, C, G, or T (which stand for the nucleic acids arginine, cytosine, guanine, and thymine). For comparison, the King James Bible contains only 3,116,480 letters.

Many have argued that the probability of that many letters arising in the proper order by chance or natural selection is exceedingly low. Some scientists, on the other hand, point to experiments that created the building blocks of the DNA spine and the four nucleic acids, and posit that this shows the final DNA molecule could occur by biochemistry alone.

I personally have a hard time believing that. First, I can only find three such experiments reported in the literature. One was discovered to be a fraud more than a decade after its publication. Second, the latter two have yet to be replicated by other researchers (as far as I can find in 2018). Third, the conditions for creation of the DNA spine required high heat and a nutrient soup, and the creation of 3 of 4 the nucleic acids required conditions that mimic the vacuum of space. Finally, though some research suggests that the first DNA came from viral RNA, the viral RNA genomes are still pretty large (3600 letters) – and the chances of them surviving and replicating without a host remain very small.

Please note here that I am not making a distinction between 6-day Creation as described in the Bible, and Intelligent Design (the concept that God created and everything in it over millions of years). These two beliefs attempt to describe HOW God made us, and not WHETHER God made us.

The bottom line is that science has not been able to come close, on the microscopic level, nor the astrophysical level, to prove whether the universe was created, or spontaneously developed.

The question on WHETHER GOD IS is currently unproved, and is likely to remain unprovable.

And even though a Rice university study[7] showed that between 25 and 55 percent of scientists worldwide see no conflict between faith and science, the atheists in the literature still claim that creation is either one or the other.

There is more. I have another couple of pieces of evidence to discuss.

---

[7] https://phys.org/news/2015-12-worldwide-survey-religion-science-scientists.html#jCp

Christ is Evidence of God

Many long and detailed books have provided evidence of the Divinity of Christ as God's Son. Because I want to talk about something else, I will reference them in case you want to read them:

- "The Case for Christ", by Lee Strobel
- "Evidence that Demands a Verdict", by Josh and Sean McDowell
- "Cold Case Christianity: A Homicide Detective Investigates the Claims of the Gospels", by J. Warner Wallace
- "Mere Christianity", by C. S. Lewis

I want to summarize C. S. Lewis's main argument here, because I (and many Christians) find it very compelling. There are exactly 4 possibilities concerning Jesus Christ as a person: He is either Lord, Lunatic, Liar, or Legend.[8]

Lunatic: Christ may have been crazy, claiming to be someone He wasn't. After all, many people who suffer from severe mental illnesses develop delusions of grandeur. They

---

[8] Lewis did not include the "Legend" possibility in his book, but it has been added since by many other authors.

attribute everything that happens to their personal mental, physical, or magical power. However, the gospels describe thousands of people, including his enemies, witnessing Christ performing miraculous healing far beyond the medicine of 34 A.D. Lunatics only THINK they have such powers. Finally, lunatics cannot return to life after being tortured and crucified. So we can rule this one out.

Liar: Christ may have been a decidedly evil con man. He may have known some amazing sleight of hand tricks, deep knowledge of herbal medicine, and an amazing charismatic presence that fooled everyone around him. We have certainly seen other such charlatans in modern history. The problem once again is that some of Christ's miracles (calming a storm with one word, walking on water thousands of yards from shore, raising people from the dead) were not possible with the medicine of the day. And once again, we are left with Christ's reappearance to hundreds of people after being tortured and crucified. It is tough to lie yourself out of being dead.

Legend: This is the trickiest one. The claim is that the gospels were written as part of a conspiracy by Jesus's disciples to play up his martyrdom. The argument goes that to overthrow the Roman and Jewish power structure, the disciples needed a hero, so they manufactured one. Proponents of this often point to other gospels, such as "The Gospel of St. Thomas," that directly contradict the Biblical accounts of Matthew, Mark, Luke, and John. According to this theory, either the whole thing was a myth (Jesus never lived at all), or accounts of his resurrection were completely fabricated.

There are several large holes in this argument. First, the life of Jesus was corroborated by several ancient historians outside of the Bible (Josephus, Tacitus, Pliny the Elder). There are also other documents that mention Jesus in more derogatory tones. But there is NOT ONE writer of the first century A.D. who denied that Jesus was a real person. The next point refuting Jesus as a legend was the timing of the other writings of the Bible. Paul (born Saul of Tarsus) wrote his letters within 25 years of Christ's death. The earliest written manuscripts of the Gospels were written about 40 years after Christ's time of death. Archaeologists and historians generally accept that legends take much longer to appear in written form. In fact, the earliest copy of the so-called Gospel of St. Thomas was dated 340 A.D. If Jesus was indeed a legend, he is the only legend in ancient times that appeared so thoroughly, and so consistently, in such a short time.

The final argument against Jesus as Legend is simply human nature. Throughout human history, legends are spread because the legend-spreader hopes to get something out of it: fame, power, wealth, or all three. The original disciples were, with one exception[9], hunted down and exterminated. No scholar has ever noted them to have gained anything from spreading the Gospel, except the satisfaction of spreading the Gospel. Charles Colson, in my opinion, said it best:

> *"I know the resurrection is a fact, and Watergate proved it to me. How? Because 12 men testified they had seen Jesus raised from the dead, then they proclaimed that truth for 40 years, never once denying it. Every one was beaten, tortured, stoned and put in prison. They would not have endured that if it weren't true. Watergate embroiled 12 of the most powerful men in the world—and they couldn't keep a lie for three weeks. You're telling me 12 apostles could keep a lie for 40 years? Absolutely impossible."*

So we are left with <u>Lord.</u> Jesus is the resurrected Son of God. The accounts are

---

[9] Historical documents outside the Bible state that John was subjected to being boiled to death in oil. When that failed to harm or kill the disciple, John was permitted to live out the rest of his live under house arrest.

accurate. And if Jesus is the Son of God, then God must exist.

Yes, yes, I know. Hard scientists don't take literary evidence as scientific evidence, much less proof.

But I have one more scientist to discuss with you. A mathematician and logician.

Enter Gödel

Many secular scientists speak, correctly, of "The Incredulity Fallacy". This fallacy states that if something is not explainable by science, it does not prove that God did it. Stephen Hawking himself used this argument to embrace atheism.

However, there is another intelligent person who had something to say about this.

Philosopher Raymond Smullyan, in 1978, published a book called "What is the Name of this Book? The Riddle of Dracula and Other Logical Puzzles"[10]. Professor Smullyan tricked me. I bought it because I love puzzles, especially logic puzzles. But that wasn't the goal of the book.

Smullyan carefully crafted several series of puzzles to help us learn the nature of true and

---

[10] ©1978 by Raymond M. Smullyan. Published by Prentice-Hall, Inc.

false statements; statements that were neither true nor false (can you feel your brain start to overheat yet?); and *provably* true or false statements. His ultimate goal was to help the reader understand Gödel's Incompleteness Theorem, and its proof. (Kurt Gödel was an astounding mathematician and philosopher of the early 20th century.) The Incompleteness Theorem states that in any consistent logical system, there MUST be true and false statements that cannot be proven.

Let that sink in for a moment.

In ANY logical system in the universe; in ANY system to which you apply the scientific method; there are ALWAYS going to be statements that you CANNOT prove to be true or false.

Gödel's Incompleteness Theorem (not a theory; a proven true statement) means it is logically impossible to explain the entire universe. Even if some basic assumptions are changed, there MUST be some true statements that you cannot prove. That gives you three choices: believe those statements to be true on faith; believe those statements to be false on faith; or choose to never decide.

For example: you can choose to accept God's existence on faith; you can choose to deny His existence on faith; or you can choose to never decide. That sounds a lot like life in the human race to me.

I will go one step further: a universe constructed with intrinsic laws that mandates faith would be entirely consistent with a loving Creator who asked us to be guided by faith.

Time for Your Verdict

So, as you can tell, I have made my faith choice to accept as true, though unprovable, that God is real, and that he created the universe. Others accept that as false – though they cannot prove it.

When I take the evidence supporting an evolving universe with Intelligent Design, add in the well-documented life of Christ as God's Son, and season with thousands of documented cases of miracles and God-human interaction – I make the faith choice and accept God as my Creator.

The rest of this book is based on that faith choice.

If you have made the faith choice that God is a falsehood, go ahead and put the book down. You probably won't benefit from anything else I have to say.

If you are undecided – please keep reading. Maybe (and I hope this) God will speak to you through the rest of these pages.

Discussion Questions

1. Do you believe Jesus is Lord, Lunatic, Liar, or Legend? Why?

2. Does someone else's doubt affect your closeness to them? How does God want us to deal with that doubt?

3. Do your beliefs usually come from your brain, your heart, or your gut? What do they all tell you about the existence of God?

God is Not a Job Applicant

So if you're still with me in this book, you're at least open to the concept that God exists. Let's get back to the question of suffering.

People complain about God when wars happen.

People complain about God when hurricanes happen.

People complain about God when disease happens.

People complain about God when their candidate loses an election.

People complain about God when someone else gets rich.

People complain about God when the bad guy wins.

People complain about God when bullies beat someone up.

People complain about God when they have a bad day.

People complain about God.

And some people conclude God isn't real.

The argument is this: "God is good. God created the universe. The universe is not all good. Therefore God either isn't good, or He doesn't exist. So, I refuse to believe in you, God. Go away. Poof."

Well, hmmm. My car is good. I can get to where I need to go quickly and easily. But my car broke down and needed repairs. Does it cease to exist?

My brother is good. But he is imperfect. He hurt my feelings. Does he cease to exist?

My employee is good. But she makes a mistake. If I fire her, does she cease to exist?

My neighbor may or may not be good. My neighbor offends me. I stop talking to them. Does my neighbor cease to exist?

God is not a job applicant. God's existence does not need our approval or permission.

Let's talk about the size of God for a minute. But prepare to have your mind stretched.

Picture a box about one foot square. Science tells us that, at room temperature and sea level air pressure, there are about 7.6×10^{23} atoms of air in this box. That's over seven hundred thousand billion billion atoms of air. That's a big number: a 760,000,000,000,000,000,000,000,000.

Science also says that there's about 10^{92} atoms in the entire universe. OK? Your brain stretching yet? That's a 1 followed by 92 zeroes. That's about a million billion billion billion billion billion billion billion times what's in our box. But I get tired of saying billion so many times, and so do scientists. So they came up with a number called a googol[11]. A googol is a number that I will never count to, because there isn't a googol of anything in the universe. A googol is a 1 followed by *one hundred* zeroes. That's a HUGE number. To reach a googol of atoms, you would have to have 100 million universes. That makes my brain start to explode a little.

And humanity has come up with an even bigger number; a googolplex. A googolplex is a 1 followed by a *googol* of zeroes. (SPLAT! That was the sound of my brain exploding. Sorry. I'll clean that up after I'm done here.)

The point is, people can imagine things that huge! We can imagine infinity! And infinity itself is a brain-melting concept! Imagine a hotel with an infinity of rooms[12], and there's a

---

[11] The website Google took its name from this number, but changed the spelling so that they could name a business after it.

[12] These thought experiments were described by Martin Gardner in his column "Mathematical Games" for "Scientific American"

person already in every hotel room. And one person shows up and says, "I'd like a room please". The desk clerk says, "No problem. Just a minute." He gets on the intercom and says, "Attention all guests, please take your belongings and move to the room numbered 1 higher than your current room. Thank you." The clerk then smiles and says to the person, "Room 1 is now open. Here's your key." Infinity works that way.

Imagine the same hotel, all the rooms are full. And an infinity of people show up and say, "We'd like rooms, please." The desk clerk says, "No Problem. Give me 15 minutes." He gets on the intercom and says, "Attention all guests, please take your belongings and move to the room numbered exactly double your current room number. Thank you." 15 minutes later, all the even numbered rooms are full, and all the odd numbered rooms are empty. The desk clerk hands out the keys, and everybody gets a room!

Infinity is Just. That. Huge!

And all that comes from the mind of man.

Now here's the really mind-blowing part: God is bigger than that.

---

magazine.

(Hang on. Got to clean up my brain. Be right back.)

God is bigger than that because He made our brains. And nothing can contain something that is bigger than it. (In the Army they have a term called a blivet: two pounds in a one-pound bag. It's a spectacular mess.)

Think of our brain as a box. If I took two boxes full of stuff and poured them into that box, they would not fit. God cannot be completely contained in our brain. It just can't. Because He's bigger than that.

And yet, the way we cope with that – is to build a box.

Rather than accept that God is bigger than we can imagine, and love Him – we build a box for Him. And we try to fit Him in the box. What doesn't fit in the box? Pshh – not gonna think about that. That's not part of God. And if it gets too hard to think about – we throw away the box. God doesn't fit, so he must not exist.

But God still exists.

Some people treat prayer like a job interview with God. They treat God like He's a job applicant. "Excuse me, God, can You prevent all suffering in my life? Can you provide me a job with $50,000 a year? Can You make sure all of the people that I don't like stay out of my way? That's where my box is. Can You fit in that box? OK. Thank You." But if God doesn't meet my interview criteria, I'm not gonna believe in Him. I'm going to fire him.

But God still exists.

God's still there; but He doesn't play your box game.

Many of us have built our own custom box: "I've got my Methodist box. In my Methodist box, God behaves this way." Over here, I've got my Baptist box. "In this box, God behaves this way." I've got my Presbyterian box over here. I've got my Catholic box over here. I got my Third Reformed Congregational Post-Millennial Church box over here. And if someone disagrees with us, we get all huffy. Because your box is not like my box.

But it's still our box – it's not God's box. God didn't give us any boxes. When we say, "Why does God do bla-bla-bla-bla-bla?", what we are really saying is, "Why isn't God fitting in my box?"

When Biblical writers wrote about God, and foretold the birth of Jesus, they gave Him all these names! "Lion of the Tribe of Judah"; "Prince of Peace"; "Son of Righteousness"; "Chief Shepherd"; "Horn of Salvation"; "God With Us"; "Light of the World". These are all boxes! Some of them are pretty big boxes, to be sure; but they are all boxes.

But when Moses asked God, "Who are you?" God replied, "I AM."

"I AM" includes all the boxes ever built. And everything outside all the boxes ever built. And that's who God is. That is how incredibly, mind-meltingly *big* God is.

And God proved that He could exceed every box because He came down to be one of us. He showed up as Christ. And said, "Yes, it is possible to love like I made you to love. Here; I'll come do it. And I'll do it when there are people who don't believe in Me. And I'll love them. And I'll do it when people don't like Me. And I'll love them. And I'll love them when they try to put Me in a box and try to kill Me when I don't fit in their box. And I'll love them when they whip Me, and they torture Me to death. And I'll love you. Forever."

So why is it so hard to put away the boxes? Because God gave us Love, He gave us Life, and He gave us Free Will to decide whether we're gonna have a box or not. Then we went off and ate the apple that says "We're like God. We have the knowledge of good and evil. We get to design the box." And we keep using that box.

Now because He loves us, and because He gave us free will, God will fill the box we give Him to overflowing. When we get up in the morning, we say to God, "God? What are we going to do today?" God says, "Well, I think we should do these things." And we usually say, "Well, I was kinda thinking we were going to do these other things." And God will say, "I'll love you; go ahead; I'll be here when you find out how that worked out."

But when you go God's way, all the rest of the things will happen. Because God is so mind-meltingly big, and powerful, and loving, knows every hair on your head. He knows the thickness of your stomach lining. He knows the size of your pancreas. He knows every beat of your heart. He knows every one of you, and He loves you more than you can conceive that love can be.

So He will fill your box; and He will stand by; and He will give you a little more (which is grace); until you finally – stop – building – the box.

How this became evident to me: I have been a lay servant at my local church for 15 years, and I love it. I love serving the Lord. It's one of my biggest thrills. And when I am assigned to speak at a church, I follow a plan. When I went through Lay Servant classes they said, "These are the plans on how to get a sermon ready." So I sat down on Tuesday or Wednesday morning and I started to write my sermon. And God said, "You want to talk about Me being too big, right?"

I answered, "Of course, Lord."

And God said, "Stop writing. I got this." And I spent a lot of the week trembling. And I spent a lot of the week listening. God kept saying, "I got this."

So Sunday morning came, and I gave the sermon you just read – essentially this entire chapter – without any notes. What you are reading now came from a later transcription of the sermon from the recording.

So hear the word of the Lord: in Matthew, the 18th chapter, Christ says, "come to Me as little children." Just say, "Whoa! How cool!" and stop trying to decide who the Lord is.

The last words Christ said in the book of Matthew were, "I got it all. All authority is Mine. Go. Make disciples of all the nations. Love them into loving Me. Do this in the name of My Father, and Me, and the Holy Spirit that's coming to you. And teach them to love Me back. And I'll always be there." He will be there in every possible way. And He will fill you, as he promised, with living water to overflowing.

I AM had the job before you started to write the job description. It is time to stop interviewing Him for the job, and let Him be on the throne.

Discussion Questions

1. What would you have to give up to accept God as sovereign? What would you gain?

2. Write down 5 phrases that describe God. Compare with the others in your group. Were there any blind spots? Are there phrases by others that make you feel uncomfortable?

3. Have you ever changed church denominations? Why? Does the reason seem important today?

Command and Control

I was a family physician for 40 years (25 of them in the US Army). In talking to young folks about going into medicine, I'm surprised at the biggest hurdle that keeps them away. It's not the memorization; it's not dealing with the paperwork and insurance headaches; it's not the long hours.

It's the yucky stuff.

I got over that in medical school, and during my medical career I spent a lot of time listening to people who want medical care. And there are barriers there, as well. To be sure, patients want healing; but they want it their way. They want to hear my advice, and are willing to give me command: "You're the doctor; whatever you say". But they don't want to give up any control over their lives. Most want me to make it better, and let them keep making the same choices in their lives – even if those choices are ruining their health.

The military recognizes this distinction. They even call leadership "Command and Control", because they realize that the terms represent two distinct concepts. Giving an order is not the same as taking over the life of the subordinate. Command is stating your will – and Control is forcing that will to be done.

The Israelites during the Exodus were desperately in need of Command and Control. They had spent generations as slaves, and although they were free, they had no clue how to care for themselves – especially in the middle of a desert full of yucky stuff.

God loved them. He cared for them. They wanted God, and they prayed for his guidance. And He delivered: manna and water. And they said, "What? No roast lamb and hummus? And I ordered wine!" They wanted God's help, but they wanted it THEIR way, not His way. They wanted His Command, but they insisted on retaining Control.

The desert is a miserable, dirty place – with no porta-potties. God, through Moses, set out three books full of rules (Leviticus, Numbers, and Deuteronomy), many of which make perfect sense to a doctor. These books go a long way toward preventing disease long before humans knew germs existed. There were rules about what they could and couldn't eat, rules on how food should be prepared, rules about what was clean and unclean, rules to prevent contagion, and rules on how to make things clean.

Humanity wanted it THEIR way; and turned these laws into rituals, often following them in their heads, but not with their hearts. And the rest of the messes of the Old Testament followed.

The problem is, the Israelites kept chewing on that Apple from the Garden of Eden. They felt they knew what was needed as much as God did. They loved the idea of control so much that they insisted on judges, and kings, and idols, and boundaries, and (for the most part) acknowledged God only when they had screwed things up.

And God let it happen, because though He was in Command – He did not wish to Control. He could have mind-controlled the Israelites to care for themselves – but what is the point of replacing the slavery of Egypt with puppetry? God gave us the gifts of free will and dominion over the Earth, and God was not going to take those gifts away. What incredible skill and love it takes to love, and direct, but allow free will![13]

Here's another example, from the Old Testament at the time of the prophet Elisha:

> *Now Naaman was commander of the army*
> *of the king of Aram. He was a great man in the*

---

[13] At this point, I expect most who have parented adolescents are nodding their heads.

sight of his master and highly regarded, because through him the Lord had given victory to Aram. He was a valiant soldier, but he had leprosy.

Now bands from Aram had gone out and taken captive a young girl from Israel, and she served Naaman's wife. She said to her mistress, "If only my master would see the prophet who is in Samaria! He would cure him of his leprosy."

Elisha sent a messenger to say to him, "Go, wash yourself in the Jordan, and your flesh will be restored and you will be cleansed."

But Naaman went away angry and said, "I thought that he would surely come to me and stand and call on the name of the Lord his God, wave his hand over the spot and cure me of my leprosy. Are not Abana and Pharpar, the rivers of Damascus, better than any waters of Israel? Couldn't I wash in them and be cleansed?" So he turned and went off in a rage. Naaman's servants went to him and said, "My father, if the prophet had told you to do some great thing, would you not have done it? How much more, then, when he tells you, 'Wash and be cleansed'!" So he went down and dipped himself in the Jordan seven times, as the man of God had told him, and his flesh was restored and

became clean like that of a young boy. –2 Kings
5:1–6, 10–14 (NLT)

You need to understand that what we translate as "leprosy" was actually a word that stood for any number of disfiguring skin diseases. After all, there were no dermatologists back then, and skin biopsies were hard to come by. For all we know, Naaman could have had anything. However, I suspect it was past yucky stuff – it was *nasty*.

Naaman wanted God to cure him, and so asked for Elisha's help. But Naaman wanted it HIS way – he wanted Dr. Elisha to pray, wave his hand, and make the rash disappear so he could get back to soldiering. He wanted to hear the Command – without giving up Control. Fortunately, his servants and advisers pointed out that taking a bath was a GOOD thing – and it worked.

Here's another example from the New Testament:

> *A man with leprosy came to [Jesus] and begged him on his knees, "If you are willing, you can make me clean."*
>
> *Filled with compassion, Jesus reached out his hand and touched the man. "I am willing," he said. "Be clean!" Immediately the leprosy left him and he was cured.*

Jesus sent him away at once with a strong warning: "See that you don't tell this to anyone. But go, show yourself to the priest and offer the sacrifices that Moses commanded for your cleansing, as a testimony to them." Instead he went out and began to talk freely, spreading the news. As a result, Jesus could no longer enter a town openly but stayed outside in lonely places. Yet the people still came to him from everywhere."–Mark 1:40–45 (NLT)

A man with a horrible skin disease (the yucky stuff again) comes up to Jesus and begs to be healed. Now according to Mosaic Law, Jesus should've stayed far away. Not only that, but healing this man outside of the rituals of Mosaic Law would GUARANTEE a conflict with the Pharisees – and Jesus was enjoying spending time loving his people by being among them.

But Jesus also loved the diseased man. He was filled with compassion. And His love left him only one option. He broke Mosaic law by touching the man, and cured him instantly.

Then Jesus Commanded the man. Sternly. "Turn away from sin. Don't tell anyone about this. Follow Mosaic Law. Go follow the ritual and make the sacrifice."

But Jesus did not Control the man. He let the man run his life. And what did the man do? He did the 1st Century equivalent of a YouTube post: "Forget the temple – go see this Jesus guy!" And Jesus had to give up the intimate, loving style of preaching – and had to start preaching to the throngs outside the cities – for the rest of His short life.

But He still loved us.

And here we are today.

He still loves us now. He is still in Command. And we – are still in Control.

In the book, "He Still Moves Stones", Max Lucado[14] writes: "Healing begins when we do something. Healing begins when we reach out. Healing starts when we take a step.

"God's help is near and always available, but it is only given to those who seek it. Nothing results from apathy.... God honors radical, risk-taking faith."

I have taken the risk, in an act of Love, to surrender my Control to God. I do not want the Apple anymore. To be sure, I still find myself chewing on a piece of it from time to time. But I do not want it.

---

[14] ©1993, 1999 by Max Lucado. Published by Thomas Nelson, Inc.

I hope I can convince you to spit it out, too. I love you, the reader of this book, and I want you to heal. I want you to be free of all the yucky stuff.

Discussion Questions

1. Have you ever been a boss? What was the hardest thing about it?

2. Have you ever worked for a boss that frustrated you? What was the problem? How did you deal with it?

3. Have you ever heard someone say "You're not the boss of me" - and then get into trouble by ignoring the advice?

Religion vs. Spirituality vs. Faith

You. The person reading this book. I love you. I love you with the intensity and indestructibility that I love Christ, and the infinity and indestructibility that Christ loves me.

That's why I'm writing this book.

But when I start to talk about faith, even with people who have no trouble in believing that God and Christ exist, there is a stumbling block that slows us down every time. That stumbling block has three sides: Religion, Spirituality, and Faith. It causes us to stumble, because for too many of us, those words are interchangeable, and mean the same thing.

I want to be absolutely clear: *these words do not mean the same thing.*

Religion is a human construct. Although the dictionary definition begins, "the belief in and worship of a superhuman controlling power, especially a personal God or gods," that is immediately followed with "a particular system of faith and worship." It is a box, with human authorities, that specifies behaviors and attributes humans must follow. Religion focuses on the rules and behaviors.

Spirituality is a human-centered search for the divine. The dictionary definition is "the quality of being concerned with the human spirit or soul as opposed to material or physical things." It focuses on an individual deciding what to do about an individual's soul. Spirituality focuses on the self.

Faith is a divine-centered search for relationship. It is defined as "strong belief in God or in the doctrines of a religion, based on spiritual apprehension rather than proof." It can focus on belief in a religious system of rules, or it can focus on the individual's relationship with God. Either way, the aim is to focus on God.

On a first, literal reading of the Bible, it is very easy to think that God expects humans to form a religion. After all, the Ten Commandments is a set of rules. The books of Leviticus and Deuteronomy, to me, read like law textbooks. And even in the wilderness of the Middle East, where the Jewish people met a pillar of cloud and fire face to face, people were still more interested in their own, material needs than they were with trusting in a Creator who had come to live with them.

The rest of the historical books of the Old Testament show consistent trends: God repeatedly stating that loving Him back will result in peace and joy, while choosing to chew on Eden's Apple will result in misery, destruction, and sorrow; Humans picking the Apple over God; and then humans blaming the misery, destruction and sorrow on God as well as themselves.

The bright shining light of Jesus Christ's life is God's declaration that the Apple is irrelevant. The rules are secondary. The game of power structures is a losing game. God would rather take all of our punishment for all of that if we would only connect with Him.

In fact, God, as Christ, did exactly that.

And then, for 2000 years, we have continued to chew the Apple, and continued to build boxes to fit God into. Even though Christianity as a faith essentially took over the Roman Empire by the 4th century A.D., we split it in two by the 11th century (resulting in the Catholic and Orthodox churches). We have been building smaller and smaller boxes ever since – to the point where there were about 1,600 Christian denominations by 1900. Current estimates that today, there are 30,000 to 43,000 religious denominations *in Christianity alone.*

God fills all those boxes out of love for that – but these are all RELIGIONS.

They are NOT faith.

They are all miniature thrones that humans sit on to tell other humans what rules and behaviors are important.

They are nouns. And they keep us away from God. And they all stem from chewing on the Apple.

I am NOT saying that faith is absent from these boxes. To do that, I would have to pick that Apple up off the floor and start chewing on it again. And that chewed-up fruit looks *nasty* from here.

What I am saying is that the box – the limitation – the religion – the noun – very frequently gets in the way of the important things. The verbs. Our relationship with God.

Discussion Questions

1. Do you confuse the terms Religion, Spirituality, and Faith? Did the definitions in this chapter surprise you? How?

2. What does the phrase "Actions speak louder than words" mean to you? Do you agree with it?

3. Is there a Bible verse that you have trouble following? Why?

Verbs versus Nouns

Ken Franklin

The Danger of the Noun

Humans are born with an innate set of brain connections that allow us to learn and process language. And development experts, after extensive research, have found the strategy that those brain connections use to develop language.

First, we listen. Then, we start making sounds (crying, then cooing, then babbling) that get the muscles of our mouths and tongue warmed up.

Next, we start with one-word sentences that indicate the important things around us. In American English, that's usually Mama, Dada, and Baba: the three most important nouns in an infant's world.

By about 2 years, we have developed a dozen or so words – parts of the body, names of pets or siblings, names of favorite toys or objects. But still – only nouns.

Adjectives start to creep in between 24-30 months, leading to two-word sentences: "hot", "cold", "big", "little", "up", "down", and the all-important "mine!"

It's not until 30-36 month that verbs start to enter the picture: "go", "stop", "climb", "move", "hop", "jump", and eventually, "like" and "love".

We are literally programmed at birth to focus our speech around nouns. Little wonder, then that we often place more importance on the nouns than the verbs.

A noun is defined as "a person, place, or thing, or the name of a particular person, place, or thing." Contrast that with a verb, which is defined as "a word used to describe an action, state, or occurrence."

Verbs are used to explain what is happening to nouns, and used to describe how nouns interact with each other. A sentence in English generally has a subject, a predicate, and sometimes an object.

I submit that one of the problems in our development as adults is that we focus way more on the nouns than on the verbs.

And by the way: "Apple" is a noun.

Let's look at an example from scripture.

> *Love never fails. But whether there are prophecies, they will fail; whether there are tongues, they will cease; whether there is knowledge, it will vanish away. For we know now in part and prophesy in part. But when that*

which is perfect has come, then that which is in part will be done away.

When I was a child, I spoke as a child, I understood as a child, I thought as a child; but when I became an adult, I put away childish things. For now we see in a mirror, dimly, but then face to face. Now I know in part, but then I shall know just as I am known.

And now abide faith, hope, love, these three; but the greatest of these is love. —1 Corinthians 13:8–13 (NLT)

To understand where Paul is coming from in this passage, let's first look at the history of Corinth. Located at the narrow isthmus of Greece, it had harbors on the east and west, making it an ideal hub for commerce and culture.

Unfortunately, this also made it a bit of an ancient-day Las Vegas. In plays written during those days, Corinthians were routinely portrayed as drunks and degenerates. Most of them worshipped the goddess Aphrodite, which unfortunately gave a stamp of approval to quite a bit of immoral behavior.

To put it simply, in Corinth, you were never expected to act like a grownup.

To Paul, this made Corinth a perfect place to preach the gospel. After a disappointing attempt to establish a church in Athens, which you can read about in Acts 17:10–34, Paul went west to Corinth and went back to his roots, making tents during the week and preaching in the synagogue on the Sabbath. Even then Paul had much more success preaching to the Gentiles than he did with the Jews, and after 18 months, he established a church there before moving on to Syria.

Later, while in Ephesus, Paul received a couple of letters about Corinth that disturbed him. Apparently, the members of the church thought they could have it both ways; they could participate in the rituals of the church at worship, and PAR-TAY the rest of the time. They were also starting to give more loyalty to individual leaders within the church than they gave to Christ himself. In other words, people were following the people that they liked, and shunning the people that they didn't like. Paul wrote 1st Corinthians to try to put them back on track.

He wanted them to stop focusing on the objects like prophecies, languages, facts, belongings, material items – the *nouns* – and to focus on believing, hoping, and loving. The *verbs*.

I enjoy reading webcomics – comic strips that appear on the Internet – and one that I enjoyed in 2010 was called "Max vs. Max" by Wes Molebash, about a young Christian man trying to reconcile his faith with his self-doubt and insecurity. (It is, sadly, no longer on the internet.) In one strip, he and his friend went shopping for new Bibles. They saw titles like the Max Lucado Bible, the Charles F. Stanley Bible, the Maxwell Bible, the Scofield Bible, the Tony Robbins Bible, the Martha Stewart Bible, the David Hasselhof Bible, and so forth. Max started noting that on many, the name of the person was in bigger print than the word Bible – as if that somehow made the Scripture more Scripture-y.

(Now stop and think – did you start to feel like I was making fun of some Bible scholar you hold dear, and – just for a second – thought about whether you were going to get mad at me? Welcome to Corinth. And how does that Apple taste?)

In many ways, we behave toward God like two-year-olds.

I mean, let's look at Exodus:

> *And the Israelites journeyed from Elim, and all the congregation of the children of Israel came to the Wilderness of Sin, which is between*

Elim and Sinai, on the fifteenth day of the second month after they departed from the land of Egypt. Then the whole congregation of the children of Israel complained against Moses and Aaron in the wilderness. And the children of Israel said to them, "Oh, that we had died by the hand of the Lord in the land of Egypt, when we sat by the pots of meat and when we ate bread to the full! For you have brought us out into this wilderness to kill this whole assembly with hunger."

Then the Lord said to Moses, "Behold, I will rain bread from heaven for you. And the people shall go out and gather a certain quota every day, that I may test them, whether they will walk in My law or not. And it shall be on the sixth day that they shall prepare what they bring in, and it shall be twice as much as they gather daily."–
Exodus 16:1–5 (NLT)

It's been only 6 weeks since the Israelites were set free from slavery in Egypt, with the parade ("you're not the boss of me, Egypt, neener neener"), and the carts laden with gold and other junk, and the herds and flocks, and the celebration, and God Himself leading them in a pillar of fire and cloud, followed by the entire parting the Red Sea thing, which to my way of thinking is pretty convincing proof that God has got them covered.

So what do we get after six weeks? "Are we there yet?" "I'm hungry." "I wanna go back and eat all the Egyptian bread and meat." (Yeah, but you were slaves getting beaten every day and making bricks outa pure mud.) "Yeah, so what? It was reeeeallly GOOD bread and meat."

So God, after smacking his forehead, sends really delicious manna down from Heaven every day. But even then, God tries to show us that it's the relationship that's important, and not this tasty pastry. (Don't gather more than you need each day.) "Why?" (Because it'll spoil.) "Why?" (Because it's My law.) "Why?" (Because I'm the Daddy, that's why! Amram and Philia, I see you – do you have some extra manna in that pouch behind your back?) "Maybe."

Do we still have that problem? Well, let's listen to some of our prayers.

"Daddy God, can I please have some wealth, pleasepleasepleasepleaseplease? Five numbers and the Powerball!" or "If You'll free me from this job, I'll never ask for anything again. Except maybe for some manna. From the dollar menu."

"Daddy God, can I have some food? Thanks! Can I have some more food? Thanks! Can I have some MORE food? Thanks! Oh, look, I'm fat and unhealthy. God, look what You made me do!"

"Daddy God, Mr. Smith was mean to me at work, and Senator Jones doesn't do everything exactly the way I like it. Would You smite them for me? Now? NOW? Have You done it yet?"

"Daddy God, I asked you to heal me and get me a raise last month. You said 'Ask, and it shall be given.' It's hasn't happened yet, so YOU'RE MEAN."

"Daddy God, I said the Prayer of Jabez fifty times in a row and got every word right and I STILL don't have that new job. I'm gonna keep saying it until You give it to me. While I'm holding my breath."

In his first letter to the Corinthians, Paul tried to explain that the THINGS – were not the point. It's not about the spiritual gifts, like prophecy, or speaking in tongues, or knowledge of certain facts. Those are THINGS. Things will all pass away. It's not about the person you follow. Individual people are THINGS, although very precious things to God. So precious that He will accept torture in your place, just like you would for your child.

(In fact, He did just that, in the form of Jesus Christ.) But we are still THINGS, and we will all pass from this Earth. What will remain after all the things are gone, all our gifts are gone, and we leave our bodies behind? The elements of grace: Faith – our awareness of God; Hope – our desire for God; and Love – our relationship with God.

Awareness, desire, and love – are verbs.

When we were young children, we were not equipped to do adult things, even when we became aware of our parents and tried mightily to be Just Like Them. How to drive a car and obey traffic laws, how to fill out a Form 1040 and pay our taxes, how to raise a child ourselves – they were as mysterious to us kids as the laws of Leviticus were to the Israelites. But as baby Christians, we don't want to do all that stuff, because it's just too HAAAARD. "I wanna be a grownup NOOOOW. Daddy God, magic everything and make it good NOOOOOW." (Which, in essence means, You be the boss of the rest of the universe, and let me be the boss of You. I'll just sit here and chew on this Apple.)

What God is trying to say; what Moses was trying to say; what Paul was trying to say; what I am trying to say; what Christ is trying to say, is: the verbs – not the nouns – are the key.

Don't sweat the things. If you'll work at being aware of God, desiring God, and loving God, you'll learn awareness, desire, and love for the welfare of each other, and God will teach you how to handle the things. Sometimes He will teach you through His word. Sometimes He will teach you through the whisperings of the Holy Spirit. Sometimes he will teach you through the experiences – the verbs – of this world filled with sinners – and saints. When you focus on those verbs – THAT is when you build what Christ, and the apostles, meant by building a church. And then you'll be ready for when that dim mirror of our Earthly eyes becomes the perfect vision of our face-to-face meeting with a God who IS ALL LOVE.

Remember when you were 2, what made everything better? It was someone loving you. It was someone kissing your ouchie. It was someone hugging you.

Love, kiss, and hug – are verbs.

God, your Father, is still offering those verbs to you. Let Him love you. Let Him hug you.

Then spit out the Apple – and love Him back.

Discussion Questions

1. If you had to choose between eating the same food for a year, starving to death, or a life of slavery, what would you pick?

2. Which is harder - focusing on who Jesus is, or focusing on how we relate to Him?

3. Make a list of verbs that describe your relationship with God right now. Are there any changes you want to make to that list?

Commit to Loving Back

The Christian path to salvation is a series of verbs: Admit; Believe; Accept; Repent.

Admit that you are a sinner, and that alone you can't fix that.

Believe that Christ died for your sin and conquered sin and death.

Accept the gift of grace through baptism or personal profession of faith.

Repent – turn away – from sin and begin loving God back completely.

(Yes, I know there is a LOT of complicated theology I am brushing over here. There is the Calvinist, the Catholic, the Eastern, the Lutheran, the Arminian, the Church of Christ, the Universalist, the LDS, the non-calvinist Protestant, and HERE WE ARE BACK IN THE BOXES AGAIN! Going over all of these theological viewpoints would take volumes. It would also give us excellent practice at evaluating and judging them against each other – which is EXACTLY what I am asking you to stop doing.)

The verb I want to focus on in this chapter is *commit*. Commit to a relationship with God that is accepting and giving of total love. Christ said it Himself in response to a Pharisee:

> "Teacher, which is the most important commandment in the law of Moses?"
>
> Jesus replied, "'You must love the Lord your God with all your heart, all your soul, and all your mind.' This is the first and greatest commandment. A second is equally important: 'Love your neighbor as Yourself.' The entire law and all the demands of the prophets are based on these two commandments."–Matthew 22:36–40 (NLT)

Not a lot of box building there. But as humans chewing on the Apple, there are many ways we can misapply even something as concise as this.

First, we can slide away from our commitment to God by becoming Performers. Performers devote themselves to constantly doing the right tasks without having to change the core of who they are. Performers try to please God with everything they do. Performers try to singlehandedly perfect themselves in order to pay back the gift of grace. Just like many people subconsciously spend their lives trying to win parental approval, Performers spend their lives trying to win God's favor. (When I am tired, Satan frequently tries to convince me that I am an inadequate performer.)

There are several problems with performance. First, it assumes there is a pass or fail. Performing requires a constant, worried push to keep from losing the gift you have already been irrevocably given. Second, performance requires a set of standards. (Standards are *nouns*.) Third, performance requires that you scour the Bible for a set of laws and follow them. However, if following laws was good enough – or even *possible* – then Christ would not have needed to be born and to die!

Performing takes our eyes off the relationship and looks into ourselves. Don't do things because you want to pass a grade; do things because you love God. Those acts of love performed by a limited human organism cannot possibly equal the acts of love of a God who makes planets with a single thought. Most importantly: performance is not what God is asking for. He is asking for unconditional, total love.

The second way we err in our love is to become Enforcers. Enforcers are people who believe that they have special knowledge of the requirements of salvation. Enforcers start their new life by embracing some or all of Mosaic Law (another noun) and then imposing it on all around them. Enforcers try to please God by passionately converting the world to those standards. Enforcers may try to frighten you toward God by describing a life without God in the most agonizing, sulfurous terms possible. (I have a personal frustration with Enforcers.)

Virtually all of us have encountered Enforcers. The historical mercenaries of the colonial era of human history were classic Enforcers. You may actually have had Enforcers ring your doorbell over the course of your life – either after visiting a church or as an assigned part of their spiritual training.

The problem with being an Enforcer is that it absolutely *requires* a bite of the Apple. Enforcement puts *you*, not God, in charge of measuring people. It again assumes that portion of Mosaic Law that you can hold in your head is the standard – The Most Important Part of the Bible. Furthermore, when (not if) people are put off by your enforcement activities, it provokes actions that are anything but love: taking offense, condemnation, dismissal, neglect, isolation, and in the worst cases, verbal or physical violence.

None of those actions are loving your neighbor as yourself. Christ accepted torture for your sins millennia before you even started sinning. You couldn't have earned it; you only have to accept it.

The third error I want to highlight is our tendency to become Gatekeepers. Gatekeepers are subtly different from Enforcers. Gatekeepers start out as encouragers, saying, "I have found something wonderful in Christ, and I want you to have it too!" They are usually much more focused on the greatness of God than on the horrors of Hell. Gatekeepers are trying to pull you toward God with the promise of a redeemed life. (I have struggled throughout this book to avoid being a Gatekeeper.)

Although the approach of gatekeeping often seems to be the opposite of enforcing, they are actually very similar in their error. Both require a large bite of the Apple. Gatekeeping requires that *you*, not God, draw the finish line that you are leading people to cross. In fact, it requires that there *be* a finish line, which is simply another word for standards. Gatekeeping puts you in charge of what sweet treats you offer to move people forward. And, finally, gatekeeping requires that you assign blame for when the finish line is not crossed - either the patronizing decision that the other isn't good enough, or the self-condemning despair that you failed at your discipleship.

Again, none of these actions are loving your neighbor as yourself. Christ did not spend His ministry on the shining best and brightest; He spent it on "the least of these."

When we spit out the Apple, we can focus entirely on the verb "to love." And in doing that, we accept that God will use you, on His terms, to build His kingdom, one neighbor at a time.

Focus versus Distraction

There's been quite a lot of discussion in the 21st century about driving while distracted. Most of the time this revolves around texting or talking on a cell phone. Of course, we were driving while distracted long before there were cell phones: Ever tried eating a double bacon mushroom burger on a four-lane highway? I've tried it. It's not pretty.

I've seen people brushing their teeth while driving; applying makeup; or reading a newspaper. Reader's Digest asked for more bizarre examples, and readers claimed they'd seen people changing a baby's diaper; changing their own clothes; sewing; knitting; and eating soup from a bowl.

We're also often distracted outside the car. Have you ever thought you were talking to someone, only to find they were talking to someone else on their Bluetooth earpiece? Have you ever walked into a lamppost while playing on cellphone or reading?

My point is, when we are not paying attention to where we are going, bad things can happen.

Let's look at three scriptural examples.

> When the Lord was about to take Elijah up to heaven in a whirlwind, Elijah and Elisha were on their way from Gilgal. Elijah said to Elisha, "Stay here; the Lord has sent me to Bethel." But Elisha said, "As surely as the Lord lives and as you live, I will not leave you." So they went down to Bethel. The company of the prophets at Bethel came out to Elisha and asked, "Do you know that the Lord is going to take your master from you today?"
>
> "Yes, I know," Elisha replied, "so be quiet."
> Then Elijah said to him, "Stay here, Elisha; the Lord has sent me to Jericho." And he replied,

"As surely as the Lord lives and as you live, I will not leave you." So they went to Jericho. The company of the prophets at Jericho went up to Elisha and asked him, "Do you know that the Lord is going to take your master from you today?

"Yes, I know," he replied, "so be quiet."

Then Elijah said to him, "Stay here; the Lord has sent me to the Jordan. And he replied, "As surely as the Lord lives and as you live, I will not leave you." So the two of them walked on.

Fifty men from the company of the prophets went and stood at a distance, facing the place where Elijah and Elisha had stopped at the Jordan. Elijah took his cloak, rolled it up and struck the water with it. The water divided to the right and to the left, and the two of them crossed over on dry ground. When they had crossed, Elijah said to Elisha, "Tell me, what can I do for you before I am taken from you?"

"Let me inherit a double portion of your spirit," Elisha replied.

"You have asked a difficult thing," Elijah said, "yet if you see me when I am taken from you, it will be yours—otherwise, it will not." As they were walking along and talking together,

*suddenly a chariot of fire and horses of fire
appeared and separated the two of them, and
Elijah went up to heaven in a whirlwind. Elisha
saw this and cried out, "My father! My father!
The chariots and horsemen of Israel!" And Elisha
saw him no more. Then he took hold of his
garment and tore it in two. Elisha then picked up
Elijah's cloak that had fallen from him and went
back and stood on the bank of the Jordan. He
took the cloak that had fallen from Elijah and
struck the water with it. "Where now is the Lord,
the God of Elijah?" he asked. When he struck the
water, it divided to the right and to the left, and
he crossed over.*

*The company of the prophets from Jericho,
who were watching, said, "The spirit of Elijah is
resting on Elisha." And they went to meet him
and bowed to the ground before him. "Look,"
they said, "we your servants have fifty able men.
Let them go and look for your master. Perhaps
the Spirit of the Lord has picked him up and set
him down on some mountain or in some valley."*

"No," Elisha replied, "do not send them."

*But they persisted until he was too
embarrassed to refuse. So he said, "Send them."
And they sent fifty men, who searched for three
days but did not find him. When they returned to*

Elisha, who was staying in Jericho, he said to them, "Didn't I tell you not to go?" –2 Kings 2:1–18 (NLT)

Elisha was focused. Elijah had picked Elisha as his servant, and his successor, at the command of God in 1 Kings 19:16. Elisha had known this, and had left everything to follow Elijah. Elisha knew he had God-ordained work to do.

So when Elijah was nearing the end of his life, and he tried to spare Elisha from suffering, Elisha stayed focused – not once but three times. "As surely as the Lord lives and as you live, I will not leave you." Now there was plenty to distract Elisha – a company of prophets was following them around – over 50 men – and kept pestering Elisha like a gaggle of reporters. "We're here today with Elisha, local assistant prophet. Elisha, we've had confirmed reports that your mentor, Elijah, is going to heaven today. What is your reaction?" To his credit, Elisha stayed focused. "Yes, I know. Now be quiet!"

Elisha and Elijah went off by themselves across the Jordan River, which Elijah parted by striking it with his cloak. (Whew. Free of the gaggle.) Then Elijah told Elisha that he could only inherit a double portion of his spirit by staying focused – which Elisha did, watching

Elijah ascend to heaven on a chariot. He then went back, focused on continuing God's work – even repeating Elijah's miracle with Elijah's cloak.

Now in contrast to Elisha's focus – the crowd of prophets, even though they were wowed by Elisha's repetition of Elijah's miracle, got distracted: "Wow, Elisha, you're cool! You're the boss! Say, why don't we go look and see where the chariot dropped Elijah off?" (Really?) Elisha tried to remind them: "No. Stop that. Stay focused. Focus on what's to come." But they pestered Elisha until, embarrassed, said, "All right! Go! You won't find anything, but go anyway! I'll be in Jericho doing the Lord's work!" And later, when the fifty searchers came back empty-handed, all Elisha said was, "Duh! I told you so!"

Let's look at an example from Jesus's life:

> *As the time approached for him to be taken up to heaven, Jesus resolutely set out for Jerusalem. And he sent messengers on ahead, who went into a Samaritan village to get things ready for him; but the people there did not welcome him, because he was heading for Jerusalem. When the disciples James and John saw this, they asked, "Lord, do you want us to call fire down from heaven to destroy them?" But Jesus turned and rebuked them. Then he and*

*his disciples went to another village. As they
were walking along the road, a man said to him,
"I will follow you wherever you go." Jesus
replied, "Foxes have dens and birds have nests,
but the Son of Man has no place to lay his head."*

*He said to another man, "Follow me." But he
replied, "Lord, first let me go and bury my
father." Jesus said to him, "Let the dead bury
their own dead, but you go and proclaim the
kingdom of God."*

*Still another said, "I will follow you, Lord; but
first let me go back and say goodbye to my
family." Jesus replied, "No one who puts a hand
to the plow and looks back is fit for service in the
kingdom of God."–Luke 9:51–62 (NLT)*

In Luke, we have an example where Christ
was focused, but his disciples were not. You
see, Jesus was nearing the end of his time on
earth, and he was arranging everything to that
end. He sent messengers to a Samaritan village
to arrange for food and rest on the way. The
Samaritans had heard that Jesus, unlike most
Jews, was preaching that salvation was open to
them! (Remember the Samaritan woman at the
well? Jot down John 4:1-42 for the story.) So
when they heard Jesus was coming, they
wanted him to stay, relax, preach, maybe do a
little fishing.

Jesus wouldn't be persuaded – he was focused and on a mission. He wanted his disciples to be focused on the mission as well. But the disciples were looking back at the long history of animosity between Jews and Samaritans, and some of them were reminded of how Elijah called down fire on people who tried to distract them. "How dare you stinky Samaritans yell at us? Hey, wouldn't it be cool if we called down fire like Elijah? Yeah, that'll scare the helmets off those Romans! Jesus! Can we smite the Samaritans with fire? Huh? Can we? Can we? Huh?"

Jesus's response was pretty similar to Elisha's: "No. Stop that. Stay focused. Focus on what's to come." And on they went.

After that, we see writings about the "Yeah–but" disciples. The first man, in verse 57, says "I will follow you wherever you go." But Christ, knowing his mind, and knowing this man wanted to be on the winning side, reminded him that the winning side was not all parties and luxury. The next man was invited by Jesus, but wanted to wait until his elderly father had passed, and the family business was cleaned up. Jesus remarked about the dead burying their own dead; in other words, "let the worldly do the world's business. Seek God's kingdom first." The third man, in a similar way, said "let me make sure everything is OK with my family." Jesus was saying, as he had said throughout his life: "If you want to serve in the kingdom of God, it has to be your priority. You can't multi-task in discipleship. Stay focused. Focus on what's to come."

One more scriptural example:

> It is for freedom that Christ has set us free. Stand firm, then, and do not let yourselves be burdened again by a yoke of slavery.

> You, my brothers and sisters, were called to be free. But do not use your freedom to indulge the flesh; rather, serve one another humbly in love. For the entire law is fulfilled in keeping this one command: "Love your neighbor as yourself." If you bite and devour each other, watch out or you will be destroyed by each other.

> So I say, walk by the Spirit, and you will not gratify the desires of the flesh. For the flesh desires what is contrary to the Spirit, and the Spirit what is contrary to the flesh. They are in conflict with each other, so that you are not to do whatever you want. But if you are led by the Spirit, you are not under the law.

> The acts of the flesh are obvious: sexual immorality, impurity and debauchery; idolatry and witchcraft; hatred, discord, jealousy, fits of rage, selfish ambition, dissensions, factions and

envy; drunkenness, orgies, and the like. I warn
you, as I did before, that those who live like this
will not inherit the kingdom of God.

But the fruit of the Spirit is love, joy, peace,
forbearance, kindness, goodness, faithfulness,
gentleness and self-control. Against such things
there is no law. Those who belong to Christ Jesus
have crucified the flesh with its passions and
desires. Since we live by the Spirit, let us keep in
step with the Spirit. –Galatians 5:1, 13–25 (NLT)

In Galatians, Paul points out that we were
freed from the world; not so that we could
continue in sin, but to follow Christ. He starts
out the chapter: "It is for freedom that Christ
has set us free. Stand firm, then, and do not let
yourselves be burdened again by a yoke of
slavery." To the casual reader, this passage is
telling people what not to do. Paul is NOT
telling us what not to do! He is warning us
where not to look!

This is an important point that Performers,
Enforcers, and Gatekeepers often miss. Paul is
not rewriting Mosaic Law; he is contrasting the
ways of loving the flesh (which distract us from
God) from the way of committing to Christ
(which focuses us on God).

We cannot follow Christ if we are not
focused on Him! Try walking down a straight

line while looking up over your left shoulder. Doesn't work, does it?

How do we get distracted in following Christ? By chewing on the Apple.

We follow our old idols. We do things because we think they're more fun than following Him. Paul lists these things in several of his letters – but I'm not going to list them here, because they are NOT THE POINT. I'll say it again: Paul is not setting up a new law – he is showing us how silly it is to go back to what we have been freed from.

We keep looking back at our old life. Christ has forgotten it. You've learned from it – don't dwell on it. Memories are wonderful – but stop agonizing over your old mistakes. Once you've learned from them, forgive yourself. Christ will lead you the rest of the way. Like the men wanting to go back to the way they had been dealing with their family – we are no longer in charge. Christ is in charge. He will show you a better of way of living where you are. And He will love your family better than you ever could. He will also probably show you how to help.

We keep watching others instead of Christ. We stop focusing on our growth when we are focused on critiquing others. Christ pointed this out to the smite-happy disciples in the Samaritan village. It is God's job to administer judgment, and He can do it far better than us, so we should just STOP. If we take on the role of arbiter, we may or may not do a good job, but it will TAKE OUR EYES OFF CHRIST – who said in John 8:11, "Neither do I condemn you. Go and sin no more."

Now I am NOT saying to completely ignore your past, or the world around you; after all, one of the things you learn in driving a car, or piloting a plane, is to have situational awareness. Understand where you are in relation to the world around you. Know where the dangers lie. But you'll never get anywhere in a car if you take every turn that's available to you. You have to watch where you are going, and you have to focus on your journey.

The Uniqueness of the Golden Rule

I want to point out one centerpiece of this passage from Paul. In Galatians 5:14, Paul quotes Christ: "Love your neighbor as yourself." The word used for love in the original Greek manuscript is *agape*. Agape is active, outward, self-sacrificing love. Remember: Christ called agape the summation of all the law and the prophets.

The great biblical scholar, William Barclay, has referred to Christ's Golden Rule as the most universally famous thing that Jesus ever said. He called it the capstone of the Sermon on the Mount; the Everest of all ethical teaching. Let me explain why.

The negative form of the Golden Rule is easy to find all over the world. The Jewish scholars Shammai and Hillel said: "What is hateful to yourself, do to no other." In the Letter of Aristeas, which describes the process of the translation of scripture from Hebrew to Greek, Jewish scholars said – and I am paraphrasing here – "As you wish no evil to befall you, do no evil to others." Confucius was asked what word would serve as a best life's practice; he said "Reciprocity – what you do not want done to yourself, do not do to others." The Buddhist Hymns of the Faith describe the same thing (and again, I am paraphrasing) – "Since you fear the rod, and fear death, do not kill or cause to kill."

However, Jesus was the first to express this rule as a positive, forward thinking principle: not "look to yourself, and avoid doing what you don't want done to you"![15]

---

[15] The Islamic Quran includes the positive form of the Golden Rule, but it originates with Jesus, whom the Quran describes as a holy prophet.

"Do to others whatever you would like them to do to you. This is the essence of all that is taught in the law and the prophets." –Matthew 7:12 (NLT)

Do you see the difference? In this positive form of the Golden Rule, we are to take the first step in loving others in the way we want to be loved. This has nothing to do with avoiding trouble, or avoiding doing the wrong thing for fear it will come back to you.

Look to Christ! Go out and do the positive, loving, compassionate, grace-filled acts that you wish would occur to you! Take action! Focus on improvement, not avoidance!

If we get stuck in the negative form of the Golden Rule, Paul warns us what will happen (Galatians 5:15): "If you bite and devour each other, watch out or you will be destroyed by each other." The negative form of the Golden Rule keeps us looking back and to the side. The positive, loving, active form of the Golden Rule – Christ's unique form of the Golden Rule – keeps us looking forward.

Christ wants us to make disciples of the world. How do we do that? Not by setting performance standards for ourselves. Not by browbeating others into accepting our judgment. Not by encouraging others into accepting our box design.

We make disciples by loving Christ back.

We make disciples by spitting out the Apple.

We make disciples by accepting Christ's gift.

We make disciples by reading His word.

We make disciples by talking to Him.

We make disciples by listening to Him.

We make disciples by living like Him.

We make disciples by actively. Loving. Like. Him.

Discussion Questions

1. When was the last time you broke a promise to yourself? How did it make you feel?

2. When was the last time you avoided an agreement because you said, "What's in it for me?"

3. Have you ever entered an agreement and have it turn out much better than you expected?

The Practice Effect

I enjoy reading science fiction. Recently I reread one of my favorites, called "The Practice Effect", by David Brin[16]. It describes a world much like Earth, with an interesting difference.

Instead of tools, clothing, and buildings wearing out and breaking down as they were used – in this world, the more things were used, the higher quality they became! A piece of flint tied to a stick, if you kept using it, would become an axe sharper than any infomercial knife!

Further, if tools were not used, they would decay steadily. The book describes feudal Lords and Ladies who picked vassals with the same measurements as the nobles, so the vassals could wear rags for the nobles' until they became beautiful – and then keep wearing them, because they would turn back to rags in the closet. The knights would beat each other's armor with wooden mallets so that the armor would become impenetrable. The vassals would live in new rough shacks until they became snazzy houses for the nobility.

---

[16] ©1984 by David Brin. Published bye Bantam Books, a Division of Random House, Inc.

Kind of silly – but you know, the same thing happens on our Earth. Of course, instead of our tools and nonliving objects improving with use – it's the living things that improve through practice.

Think about it – from the mouse traveling the maze for cheese, to the baby bird learning to fly, to the Baby human learning to crawl, walk, talk, play, sing, and read – living things learn things through practice. We've been built that way.

Paul had something to say about this in his letter to the Romans:

> *Therefore, since we have been justified through faith, we have peace with God through our Lord Jesus Christ, through whom we have gained access by faith into this grace in which we now stand. And we boast in the hope of the glory of God. Not only so, but we also glory in our sufferings, because we know that suffering produces perseverance; perseverance, character; and character, hope. And hope does not put us to shame, because God's love has been poured into our hearts through the Holy Spirit, who has been given to us. –Romans 5:1–5 (NRSV)*

In this passage, Paul alludes to the Practice Effect in his letter to the church in Rome. This church was a mixture of Jews and Gentiles who were not only amazed by the life of Christ – but by the change in the Apostles on that Pentecost where they received the Holy Spirit (see Acts Chapter 2). They hungered for that kind of spiritual life – but were unsure of how to proceed.

The first church in Rome was a lot like we are when we first approach a Christian life. They had a lot of uncertainty – What must I do? How do I pray? How do I balance justice and judgment? How do I study the Bible?

There was also fear – Will I be ridiculed? What will I have to give up? What if we get hurt?

Keep in mind that for the church in Rome this fear was very well-founded! Christ was not the only person crucified in those days – people professing belief were crucified, stoned, imprisoned (like Paul), and tortured in many gruesome ways. The church in Rome wanted to be as bold as the Apostles – but they couldn't help but notice how Rome and the Pharisees were treating them.

Paul was very much aware of these fears. After all, he started out as a Superstar in the Christian-persecuting business. We read in Acts Chapter 9 that Christ appeared to Paul while on one of these tirades (he called himself

Saul then). Saul was struck blind for three days, until Christ sent Ananias to heal him.

The book of Romans was Paul's letter to these new believers. He spends the first four chapters making the case that Christians, be they Jew or Gentile, are justified by FAITH, not by BIRTH or by WORKS. He uses the example of Abraham, who God loved for his faith – for his acting out of belief rather than simply "doing the right thing". In terms of what I've been saying, what God is looking for is our actions, our verbs, our Love. God is not impressed by our accomplishments and tasks – the nouns.

After this passage, Paul spends the rest of the letter explaining how we can evangelize through practicing the action of loving – by reacting to the world with love, mercy, and justice rather than by division, conflict and judgment.

Let's look at Romans 5:1–5 in detail:

"Therefore" – That word should be a flashing light in your Bible-study brain. Paul only used this word when he was drawing attention to a very important point. "Therefore, since we are justified by faith, we have peace with God through our Lord Jesus Christ, through which we have obtained access to this grace in which we stand."

Faith is not a one-way action. Our faith restores us to a loving relationship with a God who ACHES to be close to us. We have reconnected with the parent that we turned away from. And what do parents do when we are learning? They follow us – they watch us – they protect us. Think of the image of a parent teaching a child to ride a bike – running alongside, ready to assist. God is like a parent following along behind the baby in their first few steps[17]. The baby doesn't know it's being loved and protected – but it is. The grace is ALWAYS there. We need to embrace that grace, that peace, that protection. It's all right to try. It's going to be all right.

Continuing in the text: "We boast in our hope of sharing the glory of God." By boasting, Paul does not mean bragging – but rejoicing! God loves me! ME! Despite my past! *How cool is that*?? YAY GOD!

"And not only that, but we also glory in our sufferings..." (Uh-oh. There's going to be sufferings?) Of course! We've all had skinned knees and bruised egos. And remember, there are forces in this world that are *royally ticked* that we've been redeemed by Christ. They are

---

[17] Thanks to Pastor Glenn Litchfield for this mental image.

real – Christ confronted them – and they're still around today. More on that in the next section.

Where was I? Oh yeah, verse 3: "we glory in our sufferings, knowing that suffering produces endurance, endurance produces character, and character produces hope."

Practice takes us from "Can I do this?" to "I'm not sure if I can do this." to "I did it!" (Rejoice!) to "I can do this!" to "Pfff – I got this."

Verse 5: "And hope does not put us to shame, because God's love has been poured into our hearts through the Holy Spirit, who has been given to us."

We realize that we did it BECAUSE we never have to do it alone. The Apple from the tree of Knowledge of Good and Evil is not necessary. We need not build a box of limitations and conditions. And when we fully reach that realization – the limits come off.

In my current church, I have folks come up to me and say, "We are so blessed by what you do for this church." It happens every few months. And every time I hear it, I confess I feel inadequate.

Why? Because my faith is not great because of who I am. Let me explain.

Until about age 34, I had no idea how to visibly live my faith. In fact, I had the most practice in how to be judgmental. I was completely comfortable pointing out people's flaws to them. But God kept working on me, and I decided I would take 2 baby steps. First, I resolved to say "God Bless" instead of "Good Bye." Second, I would practice suspending judgment in others. One day, when a convenience store clerk stopped me to express how much he appreciated hearing "God Bless" every morning, it felt so VERY, VERY GOOD. I rejoiced the rest of the way to work.

Skip ahead six years, to 1995 in Columbus Georgia. "God Bless," and singing in the choir, was about all I was good at. Then my pastor called me one night and said, "Ken, the Nominations committee met – and they'd like you to become Chair of the Evangelism committee." Wait. WHAT? I knew absolutely nothing about how to tackle the job. But I prayed – and God said, "I got your back. You can do this."

I got skinned knees and a bruised ego many times, but I kept at it – and it got FUN. And that led to leading Sunday School classes. The first one I started, nobody showed. The second one, 4 people stayed with it for 3 weeks. (The third one was still going on when I retired from the Army in 2002.) I have received a great deal of practice through the Walk to Emmaus ministry[18], and Methodist Lay Servant training. It is all practice in loving.

Even with all that practice, I have not reached my personal goal. I will consider myself great at loving God when someone looks at me and does NOT say "I'm so glad you came to our church," but instead thinks "That Christ is really cool. How can I get some of what Ken has?" But I have hope. And that hope does not disappoint us. Rejoice! YAY GOD!

Remember the amazing fact of Romans 5:10: "For if while we were enemies" – while we were still thumbing our nose at God, chewing the Apple, thinking we could do everything on our own – "we were reconciled[19] to God through the death of His Son" – how mind–boggling a concept both then and now! – "much more surely, having been reconciled, will we be saved by His life." Which is easier? Dying for an enemy or loving a friend?

Christ has already done the hard part. After suffering and dying for us – how hard is

---

[18] emmaus.upperroom.org

[19] "To reconcile" means "to restore friendly relations between; to cause to coexist in harmony".

sticking around to love the faithful? "Pfff – I got this."

Think about every 12-step recovery program for physical and psychological addiction. The medical research is clear: what works best is establishing faith, then practicing that faith, then putting it into action as the practice effect takes over. In fact, it's practically the only thing that works at all.

Verbs change nouns. Relationships change people. Verbs are more powerful than nouns.

Control, Hate, Insult, and Judge are verbs. Verbs born of the Apple.

Love, Heal, Support, Listen, and Encourage are verbs. Verbs born of our Creation.

You get good at what you practice.

The way to become controlling is to insist on control. The way to get good at hating is to hate. The way to get good at insulting is to insult. The way to become judgmental is to judge.

None of those will get you good at loving.

The way to become loving is to love. The way to become healing is to heal. The way to become supporting is to support. The way to become a listener is to listen. The way to become an encourager is to encourage.

The way to become a follower is to follow. The way to become a disciple is to discipline yourself. The way to become a lover of humanity is to love.

So what other verbs does this practice effect work on? Here are some examples:

Pray – don't know how? Just do it! Get help from your pastor – or a friend – or from the Psalms – or from Christ's pattern that we repeat every week. It gets easier.

Study – don't know how to understand the Bible? Just do it! Ask your pastor or your friends for study guides that have helped them. Look at *The Upper Room* or *Our Daily Bread* on the internet for study guides. It gets easier.

Show mercy – don't know how? Just do it! Forgive the next person who ticks you off or hurts your feelings. Give them a wave and a smile instead of a fist and finger. Feeling hurt? Get a hug from a friend instead of a baseball bat from the closet. It gets easier!

Seek justice – don't know how? Just do it! Practice thinking and praying before you act. Read your instruction manual – the Bible. The right choice will give you God's peace – and remind you that He's with you. You will act with justice – and it gets easier!

Speak truth – Don't know how? Just do it! Don't repeat gossip and rumor. Investigate the truth before you speak, and have it ready. Listen to people – especially, not just those who think just like you. It gets easier! You will see.

Rejoice – constantly! Don't know how? Just do it! I mean – have you seen the size of our larger-than-googolplexes God? Do you know how amazingly awesome He is? Rejoice! It gets easier!

And now back to the most excellent way:

Love – EVERYONE. Don't know how? Just do it! Go up to someone in the opposite political party, or someone that has offended you, or someone who repulses you – and say something nice to them. Even if it's just a sincere "God Bless." It gets easier!

And when life presents struggles – and it always will – keep practicing. God is right beside you! We have been reconciled to him! His presence and love is there to fuel your hope. That hope does not disappoint us! REJOICE!

Discussion Questions

1. What is the difference between forgiving and enabling?

2. What discipleship verb do you need more practice at? What skill have you improved at the most?

3. Have you ever made it hard for someone else to persevere? If so, what did you to to resolve that problem, if anything?

The Eternal Opponent

Ken Franklin

Loving in Noise and Traffic

"Sir," the woman said, "you must be a prophet. So tell me, why is it that you Jews insist that Jerusalem is the only place of worship, while we Samaritans claim it is here at Mount Gerizim, where our ancestors worshiped?" Jesus replied, "Believe me, dear woman, the time is coming when it will no longer matter whether you worship the Father on this mountain or in Jerusalem. You Samaritans know very little about the one you worship, while we Jews know all about him, for salvation comes through the Jews. But the time is coming—indeed it's here now—when true worshipers will worship the Father in spirit and in truth. The Father is looking for those who will worship him that way. For God is Spirit, so those who worship him must worship in spirit and in truth."

The woman said, "I know the Messiah is coming—the one who is called Christ. When he comes, he will explain everything to us."

Then Jesus told her, "I AM the Messiah!" —
John 4:19–26 NLT

As I'm sure you have no doubt learned, just because you have given your life to Christ (or maybe, BECAUSE you have given your life to Christ), life does not immediately become perfectly joyful, perfectly serene, or perfectly painless. Once you fully accept a loving relationship with God, you strive and desire a life where you can love him back – worship Him – in Spirit and in Truth. The Holy Spirit provides the Spirit, and loving Him back reveals the Truth.

In the 21st century, the majority of the world is NOT a place of Spirit and Truth – in fact, as I write this, many people claim America is living in the "Post-Truth Era.[20]" This means that Worshipping in Spirit and in Truth feels more like Worshipping in Noise and in Traffic.

Of course, Noise and Traffic are nothing new. David was chosen by God to be King, and spent most of his life dealing with problems. He had to fight a giant as a teenager! (See 1 Samuel 17.) He gave up his life and his family to play harp to cure Saul's depression (See 1 Samuel 16:14–23) – only to have Saul use him for spear target practice (See 1 Samuel 18:10–11)! He fought dozens of battles for Israel,

---

[20] Post-truth politics (also called post-factual politics and post-reality politics) is a political culture in which debate is framed largely by appeals to emotion disconnected from the details of policy, and by the repeated assertion of talking points to which factual rebuttals are ignored.

usually followed by hiding in caves to avoid assassination by his fellow countrymen! Even after he was king, he faced a rebellion and uprising by one of his sons, Absalom! (Let me tell you, 1st and 2nd Samuel have WAY more intrigue than "The Young and The Restless".) But through it all – even after he broke his faith with God – David continued to worship.

Even Christ had to endure interruptions. In the New Testament, Christ and the disciples dealt with interruptions all the time. Matthew 14 tells us that shortly after hearing that his cousin, John the Baptist, had been beheaded by Herod Antipas, Jesus went off in a boat in an effort to have some time alone. The local needy would have nothing of it; a crowd of 5000 was there when he landed. so Christ spent the day healing them, and then created a fish buffet from five loaves and two fishes. Later, in Gennesaret, they went to teach – and ended up running clinics.

So noise and traffic are inevitable on this world, even to the faithful. Let's figure out how to understand it – and how to deal with it. I'd like to offer you four simple conclusions we can pull from the Bible.

Christ is Real – so Satan is Real

The Gospels have several references of Jesus encountering and describing Satan.

First, look at Jesus' time being tempted in the wilderness shortly after he was baptized. (See Matthew 4:1–11, Mark 1:12–13, and Luke 4:1–13.) Please keep in mind: none of his disciples went with Jesus on this trip. In fact, none of them had been selected yet! The only way this even could find its way into the Bible would be for an eyewitness to tell it to the Apostles. And their only eyewitnesses were Jesus and Satan. Therefore, this description of Satan came from Christ Himself.

There are other instances of Christ describing Satan as a real entity. In Matthew 12:26 and Mark 3:23, Christ responded to Pharisees who claimed that He was empowered by Satan: "...if Satan is casting out Satan, then he is divided and fighting against himself. His own kingdom will not survive." In Matthew 16:22–23, Peter tried to reassure Jesus that He did not have to suffer and die. This was so similar to Jesus's temptation in the wilderness that He replied, "Get away from me, Satan! You are a dangerous trap to me." Jesus loves the disciples – but His commitment to his mission kept Him headed toward the cross.

Let me give you a personal example of the reality of spiritual evil on this earth. Back in 1984, after several years of falling away from Christ, Terri and I made a commitment to baptism by immersion[21]. The date was set two weeks later. And over the next 10 days, you would be AMAZED at the number of emergencies and problems that came up: problems with our house, problems at our workplaces, problems with Matt's babysitter. And 36 hours before the baptism, we started to wonder if we shouldn't put it off a while. But we prayed, and said: NO. We must keep our commitment to God. And over the next 24 hours, with NO ACTION FROM US, every one of those crises evaporated.

If I'm nuts – then the Bible is nuts. (I'm either a Liar, Loony, Legend, or Liturgist. You have to decide.) I can't pretend that I've seen a demon face to face any more than I've touched Jesus' cloak. But these experiences happen to people every day, and are no more fanciful than the New Testament. So – accept the fact that Satan hates you for loving God, and he can provide real, tangible trouble for you.

God Is In Control – so You Are NOT In Control

How do I know this? Read the entire Old Testament. Every time people tried to run

---

[21] We had both been baptized by sprinkling as infants, and while the churches of our parents felt that was sufficient, the church we were attending at that time felt that immersion was the only TRUE baptism. I am not going to give you a pronouncement on this issue, because that requires Apple-chewing. Our goal was rededicating ourselves fully to God through Christ.

things with judges, or kings, or armies, or committees, or Sanhedrins – IT GOT MESSED UP. Every time someone followed God's will – miracles happened.

Do you have free will? You betcha. In his great devotional, "My Utmost for His Highest[22]", Oswald Chambers wrote, "When I stand face to face with Jesus Christ and say, 'I will not obey,' He will never insist. But when I do this, I am backing away from the re-creating power of His redemption." William Paul Young, author of "The Shack", puts it in a more modern context:

> "Every morning, I get up and pray, 'God, what are we going to do today?' And God says, I think we should do this and this and this.' Then I pray, 'That's cool, but I was thinking I should do this and this and this.' Then God says, 'Well, OK, but don't expect me to help you do it."

Trust in God is entirely different from trust in another human being. When you, an Apple-chewing person on your throne, follow yourself or another Apple-chewing person, what happens is the result of both your fallible efforts, with the occasional life-saving grace of God the spectator staying close. But when you

[22] Original ©1935 by Dodd, Mead & Company. ©1963, 1992 by Oswald Chambers Publications Association, Ltd. 2010 version published by Discovery House.

spit out the Apple and trust in the guy who built the planet, you will achieve things that you could NEVER achieve on your own. And THAT is when people around you will notice God through you. Especially if you give Him the credit.

You Can't Do It Alone

Satan's strategy is to use the forces of every single demon, and every Apple-chewer to remind you of how fallible you are, and to make sure you fail.

Wait – demons? You didn't say there would be demons!

Well, demons are there in the Bible. Christ referred to them several times, both as He was casting them out of people, and as He was answering the charges of the Pharisees. Also remember that Paul referred to them in scripture, for example:

> *For we are not fighting against flesh-and-blood enemies, but against evil rulers and authorities of the unseen world, against mighty powers in this dark world, and against evil spirits in the heavenly places. –Ephesians 6:12 (NLT)*

Satan's number one trick since the beginning of humanity has been to tell you that you are "just like God" – and then demonstrate that you're not.

Every person who has felt so despondent that they chose suicide has internalized a feeling of having power; of failing with that power; and feeling completely alone. Every recovering alcoholic and addict has felt that complete sensation of aloneness. Every person on the brink of self-destruction has decided that they can't do it alone. And Satan likes it that way.

And you know what? In this, Satan is right.

You can't do it alone.

Satan is bigger than you. He's got more bad guys than you've got strength and smarts.

You can't do it alone.

BUT YOU ARE NEVER ALONE.

God gave you the gift of love when He made the world. God loved you before He created the universe. God is so big that He knew your entire DNA structure before the Big Bang. God made this entire planet so that He could have a loving, face-to-face relationship with you. And He is always present and near to you. Yes, He will not control you; but He will add his strength to yours whenever you lovingly choose to use it.

And God is way bigger than Satan. And Love is a tool Satan cannot overcome – as long as you hold on to it.

God is Love. So First, Love.

So, we now know what the battleground is. We know who our opponent is. We know who our leader is. And we know that we have a permanent place in His Army. So, what are our marching orders? How do we deal with the noise and traffic?

God is Love. Agape. Caring more for others than yourself. Lifting up everyone around you regardless of the circumstance.

So this leads to our final Biblical conclusion: First, Love. If someone interrupts you: LOVE. If someone insults you: LOVE. If someone fails to meet your expectations: LOVE. If you hear a rumor or gossip: LOVE. If you disagree with another believer: LOVE. If you start with love, and grow daily in God, you and God will find the solution. If you start with self, chew on the Apple, and stay in the world that you had before Christ, the solution will evade you.

So let's summarize:

Christ is real, so Satan is real. Get used to it.

God is in control, so you are not in control. Practice it.

You can't do it alone. But, you're not alone. Hallelujah.

God is Love, so First, Love. Always.

It can't be that simple; can it?

Well, it's not that simple. You've heard it said, "The devil is in the details."

(By the way, did you know that the original quote, by Gustave Flaubert, was "God is in the details"? I wonder how it got changed? Hint: it involves bad guys we can't see.)

Remember that every day of your life is an open–book exam with God as your study partner, and millions of other believers who want to study alongside you: studying the Bible, serving the community, learning in groups, and worshipping as part of a church body.

You – with Him – can do this.

Discussion Questions

1. Do you believe Satan is a real spiritual being? Why or why not?

2. Have you ever felt you were under spiritual attack? If so, how did you deal with it?

3. How does giving up control make you feel?

Punching Jesus in the Face

By the humility and gentleness of Christ, I appeal to you—I, Paul, who am "timid" when face to face with you, but "bold" toward you when away! I beg you that when I come I may not have to be as bold as I expect to be toward some people who think that we live by the standards of this world. For though we live in the world, we do not wage war as the world does. The weapons we fight with are not the weapons of the world. On the contrary, they have divine power to demolish strongholds. We demolish arguments and every pretension that sets itself up against the knowledge of God, and we take captive every thought to make it obedient to Christ. And we will be ready to punish every act of disobedience, once your obedience is complete.

You are judging by appearances. If anyone is confident that they belong to Christ, they should consider again that we belong to Christ just as much as they do. So even if I boast somewhat freely about the authority the Lord gave us for building you up rather than tearing you down, I will not be ashamed of it. I do not want to seem to be trying to frighten you with my letters. For some say, "His letters are weighty and forceful, but in person he is unimpressive and his speaking amounts to nothing." Such people should realize that what we are in our letters when we are absent, we will be in our actions when we are present. We do not dare to classify or compare ourselves with some who commend themselves. When they measure themselves by themselves and compare themselves with themselves, they are not wise. We, however, will not boast beyond proper limits, but will confine our boasting to the sphere of service God himself has assigned to us, a sphere that also includes you. We are not going too far in our boasting, as would be the case if we had not come to you, for we did get as far as you with the gospel of Christ. Neither do we go beyond our limits by boasting of work done by others. Our hope is that, as your faith continues to grow, our sphere of activity among you will greatly expand, so that we can preach the gospel in the regions beyond you. For we do not want to boast about work already done in someone else's territory. But, "Let the one who boasts boast in the Lord." For it is not the one who commends himself who is approved, but the one whom the Lord commends. −2 Corinthians 10 (NLT)

I have a question for you. Do you know someone, either on TV or in real life, that you "love to hate"? You know the type; a character in a long-running TV show that is so very obnoxious that you can't take your eyes off them?

Another question: do you LOVE a good argument? Sometimes it doesn't matter what the argument is about. You really want to be seen – and HEARD – as right. Or maybe, you don't care who's right – you just enjoy the arguing!

Well, if you're one of those people, you would have LOVED Corinth in the first century AD. Corinth was like New York City, Los Angeles, and Las Vegas compressed into a ball and allowed to explode. The city was wealthy; it attracted the famous and noble; you could find a place to buy just about any item (and any experience); and it loved to hear new ideas.

Well, into this city comes Paul, the man who went from torturing Jesus's followers to advocating for him with all his heart. The Pharisee who became an Apostle. What a story he had to tell! So Paul and his fellow disciples founded a church there. He spent 18 months there. He lived and explained Jesus's teachings. And then moved on to spread the gospel elsewhere. And the Christian church in Corinth transformed the city into a beacon of holiness.

Except, weeeeellllllllllllllll, not exactly.

You see, the people of Corinth couldn't quite shake their previous habits. It wasn't enough to embrace the idea of Christianity – they had to market it. And by marketing, I mean marketing themselves as the best influencer of it. So the church became fractured by speakers and followers deciding who made the best teaching points, and had the most attractive ideas, and they split into groups following the popular speakers rather than the Christ they were talking about.

They were putting themselves in charge.

They were chewing on the Apple.

Not only that, but look at verse 1 again: "By the humility and gentleness of Christ, I appeal to you–I, Paul, who am 'timid' when face to face with you, but 'bold' toward you when away!" Paul was trying to make the message about God and Christ, and not about him. However, people took his timidity as weakness. So Paul sat in prison for his faith while Corinthians were lounging and eating grapes, and being entertained by flashy speakers. No wonder he felt he needed to be bold; he had to get their attention back!

In fact, Paul took quite a bit of offense at this practice. In verses 4–6 he says, "The weapons we fight with are not the weapons of the world. On the contrary, they have divine power to demolish strongholds. We demolish arguments and every pretension that sets itself up against the knowledge of God, and we take captive every thought to make it obedient to Christ. And we will be ready to punish every act of disobedience, once your obedience is complete."

Paul felt that Christ had given him the authority to smack down these speakers that put their own importance above the importance of the undiluted word of God. And he said in no uncertain terms that he would do so. But – he attached a condition to it: "Once your obedience is complete." In other words, he gave everyone in Corinth a chance to turn back to God's truth and Christ's grace, and away from their worship of their own points of view. Paul did not want it to appear to be "Paul's way or the highway," because then he would be making the same mistake as those he took offense to.

I want you to imagine the human being that you love and admire the most standing next to you, in front of a group of other people. And you point out the wrongdoings that you have heard about every person in that audience. And then you find out that the friend next to you has personally signed a contract with each member of the group. A contract agreeing to take the blame for every single thing they did wrong.

Now imagine that you are given a blindfold, and each person is brought before you, and you punch each of those sinners in the face for what they did. And then you take off the blindfold and see everyone unharmed – except your best friend, who is battered and bloodied. By you.

Now imagine Paul coming into Corinth with all his holy righteousness and a big stick: I can't STAND it when people say 'Christ will grant me everything I want and make me rich and famous!' WHACK! 'It makes my blood boil when you say, 'Christ forgives all sin, so I can do anything I want and Christ will forgive me!' WHACK! 'Christ will stop loving you if you don't follow every single commandment the way I think you should!' WHACK!

Then Christ steps forward, having taken every blow Paul dished out.

Christ says, "Why are you persecuting me?"

Paul says, "I'm not, Christ, I'm attacking those who aren't following you."

Christ, bleeding and broken again, replies, "But I died for them. I redeemed them. I love them. When you attack them, you're not loving Me – you're attacking Me."

Paul, realizing his error, drops the stick. He says, "Oh, Lord – I'm so sorry. I didn't mean to hurt You. I love You."

"It's all right, Paul," Jesus says tenderly. "I love you, too. I've been through much worse. But I'd like you to stop, please."

Paul didn't do that, of course. You see, Paul recognized that the exercise of power is Satan's game. God's more excellent way is the exercise of love, rather than the exercise of power. It gets back to that Apple in the Garden of Eden. That apple was from the Tree of Knowledge of Good and Evil – not the Tree of Intelligence. The fruit of that tree has NOT led us to be smarter. It has led us to be really good at fences – and fenses. And no, that's not a spelling error.

We take of<u>Fense</u>. We do it *so* very easily. And it sets us off, and makes us say things we often regret later. Or – even worse – it leads to bitterness that makes forgiveness, connection, and love harder with every word we speak.

And Satan laughs. It's like the Mr. Burns in the Simpsons says. "Excellent. Everything is going according to plan."

And Jesus weeps. Because every harsh, unloving word we unleash – is a punch in Christ's face.

Now, it is perfectly all right to mourn behavior of those who hurt you. Christ said, "Blessed are those who mourn." But it is *not* all right to attack them. Christ *never said*, "Blessed are those who attack in My name."

What Christ wants us to do is spit out the Apple. But it feels too good to stay in command.

So our next strategy is to build a fence. The great De<u>Fense</u>. You've seen the justifications:

"I don't need that kind of negativity in my life."

"I'm afraid that if I reach out, I'll get attacked again."

"I'll pray for you," which means, "I'll pray that God lets you see exactly what a jerk you are."

And instead of a church – a community – a nation – a fellowship, we get a political party – a faction – a clique – a loner – and a sufferer.

And Satan laughs. "Excellent."

And Jesus weeps. Because every fence we build – is a barrier between us and His kingdom. Christ will always stay on the other side of every fence you build, because God gave you free will. Christ will stay right beside it, ready to help you tear that fence down; but you have to use your free will to tear it down, and you have to stop building new ones.

You can read in the rest of 2 Corinthians 10 – and throughout the rest of Paul's letters – that Paul personally struggled with these same 'fenses and fences'. He often laid down rules on how Christians should worship; however, these threatened to replace Moses's laws with Paul's laws. But if we read all of Paul's letters, we see that Paul recognized these faults in himself. Look at verse 12: "We do not dare to classify or compare ourselves with some who commend themselves. When they measure themselves by themselves and compare themselves with themselves, they are not wise." In other words, it's not about who is the best ambassador for Christ. The judgment we gain from the Apple is worthless.

It's about Christ.

It's about loving Him with all your heart, and all your mind, and all your soul, and all your strength. Practice it. You'll get better at it.

It's about loving Him back by caring for yourself the way Christ would care for you. Loving Him back by working on your own personal holiness. Practice it. You'll get better at it.

It's about loving Him back by loving every single other human being the way Christ would care for you. Practice it. You'll get better at it.

Because every time you shut others out; every time you attack others; you are attacking Christ. He's tough – He's dealt with worse – He gets hurt like that EVERY DAY – and yet He loves us. Doesn't someone that astoundingly good deserve our best possible love?

Billy Graham said it very well: "It is the Holy Spirit's job to convict, God's job to judge, and my job to love." But I do not follow Billy Graham. I follow Christ.

For those of you who don't feel you have that close a relationship with Christ: please talk to God about it. He'll listen. Christ has such an amazing gift to offer you.

Accept His gift of infinite love and forgiveness.

Turn away from a life of Fences, Offenses and Defenses.

Accept a relationship with Him as the guiding center of your existence.

You will be astounded at the life you will gain.

And as for those of you who have already stated your commitment to Christ:

Go. Love.

"But what about…" No. You're about to slap Jesus.

Spit out the Apple.

Love.

"But when they do…" No. You're about to punch Jesus.

Love. God's got the rest.

Spit out the Apple.

Love.

Discussion Questions

1. If Jesus appeared in front of you, and hugged someone you really don't like before He hugged you, what feelings would you experience? What would you do?

2. Are there any unrepentable sins? If so, what are they?

3. How could you convince a group you've hurt that you have truly changed in your attitude toward them?

The Enemy's Quiver of Weapons

From 1993-2000, I was a member of Striplin Terrace United Methodist Church in Columbus, Georgia. It was relatively small, but a loving and welcoming church. Terri and I attended Sunday School regularly and went through several books that provoked a lot of loving, thoughtful discussion and spiritual growth.

One of those books was "Satan's Whispers: Breaking the Lies that Bind" by Robert Don Hughes[23]. I still have my copy. Whenever I feel attacked, or see someone I care about getting attacked, I often refer to it.

This book has already addressed some of the strategies that Satan and his forces use to pry people away from God's love. (I used to say "minions" instead of "forces", but I somehow can't see the little yellow dudes from the "Despicable Me" movie serving Satan.) Specifically, the whispers that "God doesn't exist", "Satan doesn't exist", "God doesn't live

---

[23] ©1992 by Robert Don Hughes. Published in 1992 by Boardman Press and again in 2006 by Wipf and Stock Publishers.

up to our standards", and "The Apple makes us like God" have been covered so far. Some of Satan's other sneaky tricks, however, deserve a closer look.

Go Ahead and Sin! You'll Be Forgiven...

This lie states that our secret sins, the ones we do with our Web Browser history turned off, the ones we do when nobody else is watching, are all OK. This lie is usually followed up by, "Even if I get caught, Jesus died for it anyway, so I'll be forgiven."

First, especially in the 21st century, very little can be kept hidden. People see our reactions when the subject of naughtiness is brought up. Second, sin is like salty snacks; it rarely happens only once. When we practice doing right, it gets easier, right? Well, the same goes for sin. The easier sin gets to do, the harder it is to keep it quiet. Virtually every addict believes they are very good at hiding their addiction long after everyone around them knows about it.

Finally, remember that God has never moved from a position near you and loving you – but He expects you to love Him completely, and when you give your life to Him, that is what you promise. Breaking that promise is a betrayal of love, like cheating on a spouse, or stealing from your parents.

The world implies that there are "victimless crimes" that hurt nobody but the criminal. The truth is, such crimes damage everyone with a relationship to the person committing the crime (including God). Those with a relationship watch someone they love damaging and destroying themselves. In humans, that damage leads to feelings of helplessness, inadequacy, mourning, and despair. In the case of God – well, I'm not God, and I'm all out of Apple, so I'm not going to speculate on how He feels, other than I know he mourns.

Remember, forgiveness is tied to repentance, and repentance literally means "turning away." Christ will forgive you every time you repent – but not until you repent. (I'm pretty confident God wants us to turn away for more than an hour or two.)

You Are Not Worth God's Love

This lie claims that we cannot be the object of God's love for two reasons: first, God is too big to be bothered; and two, because our sins make us unworthy of his attention.

Well, we know that there are dozens of scriptural examples that prove this wrong. The paralyzed man lowered through the roof into Christ's presence was forgiven of sins before he was healed (Mark 2:1–12); the woman caught in adultery was completely forgiven in front of an angry mob (John 8:1–11); Onesimus, a previously "useless" slave of Philemon, was praised in one of Paul's letters (Philemon 1:8–20); and… umm… there was something else… Oh yeah:

Christ was born.

If we are not worthy of God's love, then why did He come to live among us? Why did He accept the punishment for all of mankind's sin? Why did He defeat death itself?

Because He loves. God *is* Love. Love means "an intense feeling of deep affection," and the term is meaningless unless there is something there to love. The fact that the creator of the universe applies the verb love to YOU indicates YOU are worthy of receiving it.

If There is a God, He Must be Evil

This one is easy.

"How can God be real if all this evil and suffering exists in the world?"

First, humanity has been hurting each other and soiling the planet since we arrived on the place.

Second, God gave us free will, which means if we mess up the place, He will mourn, and He will pursue us, but He won't take free will away. Take-backs are a human thing, not God's.

Third, this question tries to trick us into treating God like a job applicant, which we've already shown is an Apple-chewing game. God does not need our judgment to exist.

Fourth, He showed us He was good by living among us. There is zero historical evidence, either in Scripture or in contemporary historical documents, of a single evil committed by Christ.

But God Wants You to be Happy!

"Go ahead and try it! You'll feel great! Doesn't God want you to have an abundant life?"

Yes. Yes, he does. The full statement by Christ, documented in John 10:10, states, "The thief comes only to steal and kill and destroy; I came that they may have life, and have it abundantly." That's the NASB translation. The NLT phrases it a bit differently: "Thief's purpose is to steal and kill and destroy. My purpose is to give them a rich and satisfying life."

Please note that NONE of the Biblical translations, including the King James Version, quote Christ as saying, "You will be happy," or, "You will feel good." The definition of abundance is, "existing or available in large quantities; plentiful." That does NOT guarantee constant happiness.

Joy? You bet. Forms of the word "joy" appear in the Bible about 470 times, and the word "blessed" about 300 times. "Happiness?" About 90 times. (Worth noting: "reverent" appears about 70 times, and "pious" about 20 times.)

Christ experienced life to the fullest. Christ often had moments of joy. But He was not always happy, and he never promised you would be always happy. Jesus started the Sermon on the Mount with these words:

> *Blessed are the poor in spirit: for theirs is the kingdom of heaven.*
>
> *Blessed are they that mourn: for they shall be comforted.*
>
> *Blessed are the meek: for they shall inherit the earth.*
>
> *Blessed are they that hunger and thirst after righteousness: for they shall be filled.*
>
> *Blessed are the merciful: for they shall obtain mercy.*
>
> *Blessed are the pure in heart: for they shall see God.*
>
> *Blessed are the peacemakers: for they shall*

be called sons of God.

Blessed are they that have been persecuted for righteousness' sake: for theirs is the kingdom of heaven. –Matthew 5:3–10 (ASV)

Poor? Mourning? Hungry? Thirsty? Persecuted? That doesn't sound happy and blissful to me. Showing mercy? Staying pure? Peacemaking – breaking up a fight? Those are *hard*. And yet God blesses people with a life full – *abundant* – with these experiences. And being blessed includes a great deal of joy, I can assure you.

Loving God back provides joy. Activities that celebrate God's creation and God's people are a delight. But feeling good only for feeling good's sake is NOT what you were built for.

Choosing self-destructive pleasure over the joy of relationship with God requires dedication to Apple-chewing.

God Wants to Oppress You

"Why should you follow God? He'll just weigh you down with all those commandments. I mean, have you ever read the books of Leviticus ad Deuteronomy? BO-RING. You only live once – and nobody but you knows what's best for you. Get out from under God's thumb!

It's really easy to find holes in this one.

First, if God wanted to oppress you, He could do it very easily – by not giving you free will. He can make planets and stars that run for millions of years without intervention. He has created millions of species that are interwoven into ecological balances. Look at a sunflower, a seashell, a cloud, or a centipede and tell me God can't make well-run objects that don't need convincing or oppression. Yet, God made a point of giving human beings free will. That means He designed us to choose.

Second, let's consider Leviticus and Deuteronomy for a minute. As Christ confirmed in Luke 10:25–28, the entire point of the Law and Prophets is to teach us to love God completely, and to love our neighbors completely. However, these rules were created after the entire Israelite nation had one rule of government beaten into them for generations: "Do what I tell you, and only what I tell you." Classes in civics and self-governance were not required for pyramid-builders and brick-makers. God knew this, and Moses had no desire to be their dictator – so God explained what safe, clean, considerate living should be in terms He thought they could handle.

Finally, after the nation of Israel (and later, Judah) spent centuries choosing the "You only live once" lifestyle, God choose to wipe the slate clean in the only way that could serve justice – by living, and dying, as Christ.

Loving God, and loving your neighbor, takes work and dedication. So does every other victory.

God Helps Those Who Help Themselves

This one is also known as "God Doesn't Give You More Than You Can Handle."

The whisper goes something like this: God made you. Pretty amazing, huh? But the world still has bad things happen in it. If God is *really* loving you unconditionally, then He's already given you everything you need to overcome this, or achieve this. So suck it up, buttercup! Get off your butt and solve this problem all by yourself!

First of all, the phrase "God helps those who help themselves" is not Scriptural. The saying goes all the way back to ancient Greece. Sophocles wrote in the 5th century BC, "No good e'er comes of leisure purposeless; And heaven ne'er helps the men who will not act." British politician Algernon Sidney quoted the saying in its current form in the mid 1600's, and Benjamin Franklin included it in the sayings of "Poor Richard's Almanac." (Ben Franklin was a Deist who believed that God built the universe and then stayed out of human affairs.)

There is some controversy among self-described Christians as to the truth of this saying, and many use it to argue that we would be sinfully lazy if we sit back and let God take care of us.

I believe Satan uses this sentence to drive us away from God. My favorite personal evidence comes from sidewalk research done by Jay Leno. He asked people to name one of the Ten Commandments. The most frequent response? "God helps those who helps themselves."

This is merely another trap to blame bad things on someone – namely YOU. The logic goes like this: God helps those who help themselves, so if you can't help yourself, then God won't help you. See, if this is true, then if the situation breaks you, then you're a worthless piece of trash that didn't make full use of grace. *This Is Not So.*

Remember – circumstances are *nouns*. Things that happen to you are *nouns*. Your relationship with God is based on *verbs*. The actions you take in that relationship are the keys: struggle, try, lean, ask, pray, cry, rely, cling, receive, achieve, celebrate, praise. Those verbs are all actions between you and God that reveal Him as a universe-creator who loves you by name.

You're Such a Good Christian – Don't You Wish Everyone Was?

This is the smoothest lie of all, in my personal opinion.

Friends, family, strangers come up to you and compliment you on your behavior, and what a special person that makes you. Then someone else (or, worse, some other group) is compared unfavorably to you.

"You're not like all those heathen unbelievers."

"You're not like all those hypocrites in church."

"You're not like those who don't come to church."

"You're not like those stuck-up people in those megachurches."

"You're not like all those right-wingers."

"You're not like all those left-wingers."

'You're not like all those (insert ethnicity, sexual preference, political party, or other stereotype here.)"

The easy answer, the seductive answer, is to say, "Thank you, I try." And even if you are successfully working hard at loving God back: if you don't correct the two errors in this, you can be led far, far astray.

First: it's not us or our actions that make us good. God's creation, built into us, made us good; our choices made us sinners; and Christ's redeeming grace makes us good. Should we celebrate that? Of course! So celebrate it by pointing it out every time you are complimented: "Thank you very much, but all glory goes to God." (As I like to put it, "Everything I get right is thanks to God, and everything I mess up is my own fault.") Any other thought pushes us toward the throne that God is already sitting on.

Second: the comparison is the semantic equivalent of "Want a bite of my delicious apple?" God loves every single person in the "You're not like all the" group every bit as he loves you and the person complimenting you. The loving, Christlike response is, "But I *am* like all of those people. I'm a sinner that Christ died for."

In Conclusion

Satan wants you to fail. He hates the relationship that God wants to have with you. He wants to control creation, which includes controlling you.

God wants you to thrive. He loves you, and wants to spend eternity with you face to face.

God also wants that for every other person on the planet.

Would you rather use Satan's tools to deal with the world – or your own – or God's?

Discussion Questions

1. Have you heard any of the whispers described in this chapter? Did any of them distance you from God?

2. What makes Satan attractive to some people? Has that ever attracted you or someone you love?

3. Make a list of verbs that describe your relationship with Satan right now. Are there any changes you want to make to that list?

Cans and Can'ts

By now, I hope we have established that there are three forces on the stage for the story of your life:

• Satan and his forces;

• God in three parts (Father, Christ, and Holy Spirit);

• You and the other humans on the planet.

We haven't talked about other people very much; I've saved that for the last section of this book. Before we do, though, let's compare each of these forces. Each has some innate abilities – and some innate limitations. (Wait, *what?* God has limitations? Yes – please bear with me.) Let's look at three items in the Can and Can't columns for each.

The enemy can hurt you

As we mentioned, Ephesians 6:12 says, "For we are not fighting against flesh-and-blood enemies, but against evil rulers and authorities of the unseen world, against mighty powers in this dark world, and against evil spirits in the heavenly places."

That's a lot of demons. If popular culture, television, movies and literature are to be believed, they can cause a lot of trouble. For me, seeing the verb "fighting" tells me that these forces do not have my best interests at heart. I have never seen a fight without injuries.

I have experienced such battles in my personal life (see the discussion of my rededication in "Loving in Noise and Traffic"). In addition, my wife and I like to joke about "salad fork demons". Those are the demons so short that they can only handle a salad fork instead of a pitchfork. The salad fork demons are the ones that route robot sales calls to your cell phone, put a pothole in front of your tire, misplace documents you desperately need for work, and spill barbecue sauce on your favorite tie. They usually hunt in packs, working hard to give you A Bad Day.

After one such Bad Day, I was saved by a wonderful co-worker at a clinic in Fort Benning, Georgia. Her name is Annie Ellis. Annie said, "You know, Colonel Franklin, when I have a day like that, I pray, 'Christ, I'm busy loving you right now. Would you take care of this for me, please?'"

The Bad Days still hurt. But that prayer works quite well. Thanks, Annie.

The enemy can deceive you

How many times have you been lied to? How many times have you been fooled? How many times have you learned "If it sounds too good to be true, it probably is"? Over and over again?

Again, literature, television and movies are full of stories about confidence games, betrayal, espionage, and deception. We love to watch them. We thoroughly enjoy magical illusions. We lose billions in gambling, believing that our hunger is stronger than the laws of probability. Finally, the strongest thing we have to break in every addiction on the planet – is denial. Believing the deception that we are not destroying ourselves and those around us.

Deception, betrayal, and lies – none have anything in common with Truth. None have anything in common with Christ. And they did not appear in humanity – until Eve heard the lies of the serpent and bit that first Apple.

Oh, yes. The enemy can deceive you. Christ said so when addressing doubters in John 8:44: "For you are the children of your father the devil, and you love to do the evil things he does. He was a murderer from the beginning. He has always hated the truth, because there is no truth in him. When he lies, it is consistent with his character; for he is a liar and the father of lies."

The enemy can pleasure you

Our spirit is encased in a body of flesh and blood, responding to the reactions of our brains. In that brain, electrical currents are activated by chemicals called neurotransmitters; one nerve spits a neurotransmitter out, and the next nerve takes it in, keeping the electrical activity going.

Dopamine, serotonin, adrenaline, oxytocin, and many others – these chemicals play an intimate role in our perception of physical pleasure. This pleasure can be generated by agape (self-giving love) or eros (physical love). This pleasure can be generated by chemical or electrical stimulation. It can be generated by inputs to touch, sight, smell, taste, and hearing.

But pleasure by itself has no truth value.

Therefore, pleasure can be tied to deception. All manner of destructive impulses can be tied to the concept of taking control of your life ("Nobody is the boss of me!") And then riding to the edge of losing it ("You only live once!") Of course, both of those statements deny the reality of a creator and the existence of life beyond our physical presence on Earth.

Finally, pleasure for pleasure's sake can easily lead to addiction – which steadily increases the price of that pleasure to include the loss of everything else on Earth you cared about.

Satan knows all about pleasure.

The enemy can't love you

Satan is not God. God is love. Satan is described as wanting to kill, destroy, devour, and murder. Although the Bible is not explicit about this to my reading, Satan wanted to replace God and have sovereignty over God's creation.

Sovereignty without love is control. Satan wants to dictate our action to please his own plan. Therefore, Satan cannot love you. As soon as you hear temptation say, "Look out for Number One": don't believe that you are the Number One being discussed.

The enemy can't save you - and doesn't want to

Satan has not been given power over sin and death. Christ's life proves that, because Christ underwent all the torture the world could dish out, up to and including death – and emerged brilliantly triumphant.

So as soon as you hear temptation say, "You Only Live Once": don't expect Satan to give you a do-over. He wants your Once on Earth to be short.

The enemy can't separate you from God – but it wants to (and it thinks it can)

Satan may want to take God's place – but he can't. Satan didn't make the universe – God did. God is greater than Satan.

The thing that allows me to be unafraid of Satan is that he has a huge blind spot: *Satan does not believe love is real.* He considers it a chemical reaction exactly like pleasure or pain. Thus, Satan will not take the reality of love into account in any of his schemes.

I know this from personal experience.

On July 1, 1984, two things happened to my first wife Terri and I. The wonder was that our first son, Matt, was born that morning. The tragedy was that Terri's mother, Mary, underwent mastectomies for cancer.

The tragedy was even more acute because Mary had delayed living her dreams because she always felt she had so much work to do. And because she had let the cancer go before seeking treatment, the remaining 14 years of her life were marked by pain and weakness, and her dreams went unrealized.

Fast forward to 2002: I was preparing to retire from Army medicine and work 4 days a week in a small civilian practice. I expressed a desire for us to start living out our dreams as soon as possible. However, Terri insisted on looking for full time work. I expressed my greater fear: that an illness like cancer would take her life before we could realize everything we had deferred for nearly 25 years. She reassured me; we prayed; and she began a delightful career with the American Red Cross that summer.

Three months later, my father died of colon cancer.

Three years later, Terri underwent emergency colostomy for colon cancer.

Five years after that, I held Terri in my arms as she drew her last breath.

The medical literature states there is no greater life pain than the death of a spouse. I agree with that completely.

However, before her death, Terri told her friends several things. First, she was absolutely certain of her closeness to God: "I'm very sad – but I'm not scared." Second, unbeknownst to me, she told our neighbors, and my sister, "Make sure Ken never forgets that I wish for him to find another love. He won't do well alone." Finally, during our last days, she assured me that she never doubted my love or devotion for her every day of her life.

So, here is my personal proof that Satan wants me destroyed, but absolutely can't do it: he made my worst fear – the premature loss of my wife to cancer – come completely true. And he failed to separate me from God one inch. I was – and am – surrounded by faithful disciples, and am married to my miraculous Godgift, Debi.

Satan failed.

There is nothing he can throw at me that is worse than what I have already survived. And my survival is not due to any human strength; it is completely due to the love and grace of God.

God is stronger than Satan's hordes.

And Terri is dancing and singing in His presence.

God can know you

God can – and does – know you. Not as part of the aggregate 10^{49} atoms that make up the planet. Not as part of the aggregate 7 billion people on the planet. Not as one of the faceless millions that make up your race, gender, nationality, political party, or shoe size.

God can – and does – know *you*. By name. In fact, He knew your life before He built the universe. Keep in mind that being all–knowing means comprehending space, time, and quantum possibility (whatever quantum possibility means). The Old Testament has dozens of examples of God communicating with kings, prophets, and others – and in the scripture, He called them all by name.

God can love you

God can – and does – love you. The entire Old Testament demonstrates how many times the Israelite people – the descendants of Adam, Noah, and Abraham – broke their promise to love God back. Yet God always promised to keep His side of the covenant.

Let's review the math. Since *Homo sapiens* arrived on the planet, there have been at least 10 billion people. By a *very* conservative estimate, the average human has sinned at least 100 times. As I mentioned before, that's about *one trillion times* that we have missed the mark. Yet God loved us so much that He, as Christ, survived childbirth in a stable, fleeing infant genocide, starving in a wilderness, living borrowed meal to borrowed meal, arrest by His supposed faithful, denial and betrayal by some of His closest friends, whipping to near-death, a stabbing in the side, and death by slow suffocation on a cross – as payment for YOU missing the mark.

Yeah. God can love you.

God can comfort you

God can comfort you – when you let Him. I can attest to that. And remember, I am no less of a sinner than you are.

I told you about the spear of sunlight after Terri's cancer came back.

I told you about the rainbow in response to my call to Terri.

I told you about the shouted "Yes" when I asked God if He had another spouse for me. I woke up next to that Godgift this morning.

I could tell you about the number of times I have prayed for peace after the world has beaten on me, but I can't provide evidence that proves my peace came from God. I am certain of it – but I can't prove it.

The Bible – and contemporary Christian books – are full of examples of "God things."

You don't even have to accept He is real before the comfort happens, though I believe building a relationship with God makes it easier. After all, are you more likely to receive comfort from a close friend, or a stranger?

Now, let's look at three things God won't do. Notice I didn't say *can't* do (like I did with Satan and his forces). God's ability is infinite. However, He has imposed limitations on Himself.

God won't break His promise

Even though God has infinite power, He will hold Himself to the rules he set for His relationship with us. That means when He makes a covenant, He will keep it.

If you read all of the times that "God" and "covenant" are used together in the Old Testament, you will never find an instance of God going back on His word. This is true with both blessings and curses; many times God warned what would happen if humans went back on a covenant (and most times, humans did). However, God revealed to the prophets over and over again that He was working to reconcile humanity to Him – even if that meant being Mary's child.

God won't take back his gift of free will

Remember the gifts God gave us in Eden? Dominion over the earth, and free will. That free will gift is the problem that people seem to complain about the most.

"Daddy God, make that person stop."

"Daddy God, make that person do what I want."

"Daddy God, smite that unbeliever (*unbeliever* in this case meaning 'someone who disagrees with me')."

"Daddy God, look what you let me do!"

God is certainly capable of completely controlling each of us, but then we would not be individuals; we would be puppets in a show with no audience. Puppets incapable of choosing to love. Puppets incapable of forming a relationship with God – because they are already part of God.

Satan would be *delighted* to take away free will, because control is what he wants – and loving relationships make no sense to him. But God? The relationship – the *love* – is the reason He made us in the first place.

God won't uncrucify Christ

This is the hardest one for me to comprehend; but I'm so very glad it's true.

God is capable of healing. The Bible has many examples of it; Christ attracted multitudes doing it. Christ healed hands, feet, eyes, ears, brains, and even stopped hearts. Yet when Christ returned from the dead, He still bore the marks on His hands and feet; He still had a puncture wound in his side.

Why?

Because God wants us to remember that this one death – *meant something*.

This was a punishment. A very real, painful, severe punishment. A punishment willingly accepted by the only man on record who never sinned. A punishment endured by the only human who never missed the mark in loving His Father and His fellow man.

Yes, Christ was afraid; but fear is not a sin. Yes, Christ sought another way; exploring possibilities is not a sin. Yes, Christ cried out in agony as he was dying on the cross; but feeling pain is not a sin.

If Christ's payment were erased, then the sins of humanity would NOT be erased. Those marks on Christ's body are the stamp on the receipt: "Paid In Full."

You can know

You have a brain capable of learning. Otherwise, you wouldn't be able to read this book; you had to learn language and reading as a child. Therefore, you have the ability to accumulate knowledge, and apply it to how you live your life.

This is *not* always a good thing.

In the movie "The Truman Show", Jim Carrey plays a friendly, likable person who lives and works in a small town. However, he does not realize that he has been cared for, since birth, in a gigantic TV studio visible from space! Everyone he comes in contact with is an actor; he alone believes he is in reality – a reality without television or an outside world.

In the 21st century, with literally hundreds of media sources, many people have created bubbles like "The Truman Show". These rich, complex, internally consistent bubbles are comfortable – but they shut out the rest of reality. Further, when a bubble-inhabitant talks to people who live outside the bubble, it leads to confusion, anxiety, discomfort, anger, defensiveness, or even hatred.

Knowledge is a noun. Seeking, listening, conversing, and contemplating are verbs. But while we are chewing on our own variety of prized Apple, those verbs are difficult to use. They get replaced by verbs like defending, insulting, ridiculing, patronizing, and attacking.

I find myself changing what I know with every person I meet. If you are not, you might check around for a bubble wall.

You can love

We have been made in God's own image (as stated in Genesis 1:26–27).

God is Love (as the apostle John stated in 1 John 4:8 and 1 John 4:16).

Therefore, Love is in you. It has been placed in you from your creation by the being that made the universe.

Nothing can take that away.

Can we be damaged so that Loving is difficult to do? Oh, yes. Especially by evil that values control and destruction and can't even comprehend Love.

But our ability to Love is never destroyed.

Let me reiterate: the Love I am speaking of is *agape,* not erotic pleasure (though within a covenant relationship with God and another human, such pleasure is sweet indeed). Agape, defined in Ancient Greek as "the highest form of love," is a selfless, unconditional dedication to the uplifting of another. It provides pleasure from seeing the other uplifted. The ideal of relationship, as created by God, is the free flow of agape Love between us and God, and by extension, between us and every person we encounter.

You can choose

You have free will.

God created you with it (another part of being In His Image).

Free will is necessary to create. Free will is essential to innovate. Free will is required to improve; to learn; to build; and to love completely. However, free will also enables us to ignore; to stagnate; to despair; to destroy; to forget; and to injure.

Free will is very hard to completely comprehend once you have bitten the apple.

When we choose to apply a judgment of Goodness or Evilness to objects or actions, we then immediately jump to the question, "Why?"

"Why would someone do that?"

"Why would someone make that?"

"Why would someone let that happen?"

"Why would someone treat someone that way?"

"Why would someone treat me that way?"

Once you ask the "Why" question, you are naturally drawn to form a conclusion of the "someone" based on your answer. This allows you to keep a neat Good-versus-Evil table of the people, groups, and stereotypes you can choose to form or sever relationships with.

Free will, coupled with the Apple, allows you to decide the character of God. Free will, coupled with the Apple, deludes you into thinking you have the power to decide whether God exists or not.

Free will is very powerful.

You can't make God disappear

All the free will in the world won't change existence. Most children learn "Object permanence" at about 4-7 months of age. Before then, if Mommy goes into the bathroom, Mommy vanishes from the universe. Object permanence is necessary for us to comprehend each other as separate beings.

As toddlers, we learn that we don't control the universe. We learn that other beings actually have some say in how the universe operates. Dealing with this inconvenience is why toddlers in the "Terrible Twos" can say "Go Away!" (Or worse, "You're not my Mommy anymore!")

Well, you learned that doesn't work for people. Therefore, it doesn't work for Jesus. And it doesn't work for God.

You can't make people obey God

When you make the choice to accept God's love and Christ's grace, there is a pressure to share that gift with others. When you go the next step and work on loving God back (hitting the mark) instead of continuing willful sin (missing the mark), you will start getting good at it.

But you can't transfer that skill to someone else – especially without love.

"Because God said so" is a sentence without love.

"You'll go to Hell if you don't" is another sentence without love.

You weren't forced to obey God by God. Sure, many people feel forced to obey God by religious institutions; but that path does not form a loving relationship. Rather, it forms a repressed simmering resentment that does not contain love.

God brings people to himself through a love story with Christ as the central figure. Sharing that story in love doesn't force anyone – but it works.

You can't make people obey you

Have you ever heard anyone say: "I know the answer. This problem will go away if everyone would only listen to me!" I know I've heard it, because I've said it.

Creativity can indeed come up with improved ideas for solving problems. However, improved ideas work because people CHOOSE to implement them. Remember free will? Well, every other human has the same amount of free will as you do.

There are indeed organizations and governmental structures where disobedience is illegal. However, such governments, by themselves, do not create obedience. Rather, they include structures to enforce obedience with police structures. And inevitably, in such governments, citizens choose to disobey.

Some organizations, such as the American military, do indeed require obedience. However, that obedience is chosen and agreed to by an oath taken by every member of the organization – and the oath is to the Constitution first, not a particular human. The officers are bound to be stewards of those they give orders to, exactly as much as the enlisted are bound to carry out the plans of the officers without hesitation. This is chosen obedience, not forced obedience.

God gave each of us free will – and you can't take it away.

In conclusion

The forces of evil are real, possess the ability to make you feel pain or pleasure, and can take your life. They want to divide you from God, control you, and destroy you. But they can't love you or save you.

The forces of God are real, possess the ability to love you, care about you, and save your life through the gift of Christ's grace. They can't control you or give up on you.

You, and others around you, can learn, grow, love, and make your own choices. Satan can't steal that; God won't revoke that. However, you can't choose those forces away, and you can't take those gifts away from any other human.

These three forces frame the battle on this planet. Satan wants a world of power and control; God wants a world of love and community. You have the choice to participate in either world. You were created with the tools to thrive in God's world; Satan gave you the means to live in either world, because you (and every human since the beginning) have been chewing on the Apple.

You can, and must, choose: either chew on the Apple and fail at loving – or spit it out and excel at loving.

Use the free will God (not Satan) gave you. Choose.

Discussion Questions

1. Do you think Satan is as powerful as God? Why or why not?

2. Does giving man free will weaken God? How does it affect how you feel about God?

3. What would you order everyone to do if you were in charge? Describe what happened when you failed to follow that order.

Living Without the Apple

Ken Franklin

The Value of a Covenant Partner

When a person first spits out the Apple, if they are not practiced at listening to God, a problem arises.

That problem is loneliness.

Loneliness is like drug withdrawal from the Apple.

When we first went through adolescence, we had to form our identity; specifically, we had to create our sense of how we related to the universe. And in most of us, the Apple is an attractive way to accomplish that task and get on with living. When we become the judge of what is right or wrong; when we become the "Master of our Fate"; when we make the bold step of saying, "Nobody is the Boss of Me!"; we get a short, heady burst of adrenaline, and a sense of accomplishment.

But in a healthy person, it doesn't last – because others have also decided that you aren't the boss of them, either.

Most people are social animals; we function better when in relationship with others.

Remember, we were created in the image of God, and God wants relationship with each of us. So, we interact with each other – and relationships form.

Relationships are messy, because the two people in the relationship are different. They bring different experiences, different desires, and different cultures. People vary in genders, colors, shapes, and sizes. People vary in how they express themselves, how they hear other people, and how they react to new information.

Every relationship between fallible humans includes mistakes. And how people react to those mistakes is crucial to the survival of that relationship. When we react with judgment – when we chew the Apple – we decide what the other person did, and what the other person's value is. That rarely helps. When we turn that judgment on *ourselves*, we decide what we did, and what our value is. That is also rarely helpful.

The solution? Spit out the Apple. Trust that the other person has the same value as you. Try to learn from each other in love and respect.

Will this work with everyone you meet? Of course not. Some people will choose evil; some people will continue to chew their piece of Apple; and some people will not value your relationship the way that you do.

Some relationships, sadly, will end.

But if God is involved – some relationships will start to shine.

God, the creator of the universe, built you to be in relationship – with Him, and with every other person He created. How do we know this? Christ said it when he described The Great Commandment:

> But when the Pharisees heard that he had silenced the Sadducees with his reply, they met together to question him again. One of them, an expert in religious law, tried to trap him with this question: "Teacher, which is the most important commandment in the law of Moses?" Jesus replied, "'You must love the LORD your God with all your heart, all your soul, and all your mind.' This is the first and greatest commandment. A second is equally important: 'Love your neighbor as yourself.' The entire law and all the demands of the prophets are based on these two commandments." – Matthew 22:34–40 (NLT)

Love *everyone else*? How in the world can we accomplish this?

First, love God. Accept His love, then practice loving Him back. Then, pick one person, and practice loving them in the same way. Then repeat. It gets easier.

God expressed his love for the Israelites through a special adjective: *Covenant*. A covenant relationship is one built on a promise – a trust – that the relationship is a permanent, unconditional part of your life. Remember? God has never broken a covenant. Christ made a new covenant with all of humanity at the Last Supper:

> *After supper he took another cup of wine and said, "This cup is the new covenant between God and his people—an agreement confirmed with my blood, which is poured out as a sacrifice for you." – Luke 22:20 (NLT)*

The last words of Christ to the disciples made it clear this covenant was with everyone:

> *Jesus came and told his disciples, "I have been given all authority in heaven and on earth. Therefore, go and make disciples of all the nations, baptizing them in the name of the Father and the Son and the Holy Spirit. Teach these new disciples to obey all the commands I have given you. And be sure of this: I am with you always, even to the end of the age." – Matthew 28:18–20 (NLT)*

Permanent. Unconditional. Everyone.

When you live within a covenant relationship with God, deceit, mistrust, and fear all lose their power. Instead, love and trust become a logical cornerstone that empowers you to achieve astounding things in life.

Image if you had such power in a relationship with another human being!

Marriage is a covenant relationship that binds two people with God in exactly the same love and trust that Christ modeled for us. When such a covenant is maintained, two people can be a powerful force for good – and the two humans involved get *extremely practiced* at loving other people under messy circumstances. That practice allows each member of the relationship to use those well–honed skills in forming loving relationships with others around them.

And now, I am going to walk out of the boat exactly like Peter did when Christ walked on water (see Matthew 14:22–30). Here is a chance for Apple–chewers to attack me.

A covenant relationship does not have to be between a man and a woman.

I recognize that there are scriptures describing marriage as between one man and one woman. There are also many scriptures where men had marriages with many wives, without any mention of sin by God. And remember that David, God's anointed top King of all time, had a covenant relationship with Jonathan, son of King Saul (see 1 Samuel 18–30).

In 21st Century America, there are several examples of covenant relationships. There is an organization called Stephen Ministries[24], that trains individual men and women to reach out and meet, one on one, weekly, with others who are experiencing crisis in their lives. Men meet with men; women meet with women. This is not therapy; this is being present in fellowship, love and support no matter what. I also participate in a program called Kids Hope USA[25], where a person commits to spending one hour of each school week with an at-risk elementary school student. Again, this is one-on-one; the student is keenly aware that their partner does not meet with anyone else but them. In 16 years, I have yet to see that covenant fail in making a child's life blossom.

There are a few scriptures limiting physical acts of erotic love – some between men and women, some between people of the same gender. I am not here to decide their validity, *because I spit out my Apple.*

---

[24] www.stephenministries.org
[25] kidshopeusa.org

I can find nothing in scripture that prohibits a person from forming a covenant relationship with another person in the sight of God.

That covenant of permanence, trust, selflessness, and unconditional caring is the next foundational stone you lay next to the cornerstone God gave you through grace. Living in that covenant gives us a safe place to practice honesty, openness, and vulnerability, because power and control games become meaningless. Practicing honesty, openness, vulnerability, and the benefits of agape love empowers both partners to change the world around them.

Discussion Questions

1. Describe the difference between a promise and a covenant.

2. Did anyone ever break a covenant between you? Describe how it made you feel. Does God feel that way when we sin?

3. What obstacle could you conquer if you were *certain* you could count on another person?

The Value of Small Groups

Two people are better off than one, for they can help each other succeed. If one person falls, the other can reach out and help. But someone who falls alone is in real trouble. Likewise, two people lying close together can keep each other warm. But how can one be warm alone? A person standing alone can be attacked and defeated, but two can stand back-to-back and conquer. Three are even better, for a triple-braided cord is not easily broken. –Ecclesiastes 4:9–12 (NLT)

We have discussed the value of a covenant partner. As King Solomon wrote in the passage above, two together are better than one.

But then Solomon tossed off this gem: "Three are even better, for a triple-braided cord is not easily broken." Some Bible commentators suggest that by three, Solomon meant two people with God present. However, most agree that Solomon was referring to three humans working together toward a common goal.

The strength of three is seen in engineering. A triangular shape is the most stable rigid structure. That's why girder bridges have each square divided in two with a diagonal cross-brace. And, as Solomon pointed out, braided cords of three or more strands are much stronger than three strands simply lying next to each other.

In human interactions, three people working together in love and trust can be quite powerful. If two start to disagree, the third can help the other two regain their perspective and come to understanding. However, if two people turn to the third as a judge between the two of them, or if two choose to judge the third for some misdeed or slight – that group can self-destruct in many spectacular and painful ways.

How to avoid this? Oh, yeah – did you see what I did? If two demand that the third use the "gift" of judging right from wrong, or if two decide to share that Apple between them... disaster happens. The key is that this small group must connect regularly and practice supporting, listening, and caring. The group must trust each other enough to practice honesty, openness, and vulnerability in order to remain cohesive and effective.

Does this small group have to be exactly three? Of course not. Sociologists and theologists have studied this, and in the context of mutual support and lasting relationships, the ideal number is 5-7. Less, and the group can fall apart when people have to miss meetings for the demands of life. More, and there is a risk of one or more feeling left out of the discussion – and the caring.

There is a key additional ingredient necessary for a small group to remain holy and effective. The trustworthiness must include respect for privacy. In this open, honest, and vulnerable relationship, social intimacy is inevitable. Members will share things about themselves that can only be understood within the group. Outside the group are a lot of apple-chewers, and sharing of such intimate information is called gossip. The Bible has a lot to say about gossip:

> *Dear brothers and sisters, not many of you should become teachers in the church, for we who teach will be judged more strictly. Indeed, we all make many mistakes. For if we could control our tongues, we would be perfect and could also control ourselves in every other way. We can make a large horse go wherever we want by means of a small bit in its mouth. And a small rudder makes a huge ship turn wherever the pilot chooses to go, even though the winds are strong. In the same way, the tongue is a small thing that makes grand speeches. But a tiny spark can set a great forest on fire. And*

among all the parts of the body, the tongue is a flame of fire. It is a whole world of wickedness, corrupting your entire body. It can set your whole life on fire, for it is set on fire by hell itself. People can tame all kinds of animals, birds, reptiles, and fish, but no one can tame the tongue. It is restless and evil, full of deadly poison. Sometimes it praises our Lord and Father, and sometimes it curses those who have been made in the image of God. And so blessing and cursing come pouring out of the same mouth. Surely, my brothers and sisters, this is not right! Does a spring of water bubble out with both fresh water and bitter water? Does a fig tree produce olives, or a grapevine produce figs? No, and you can't draw fresh water from a salty spring. –James 3:1–12 (NLT)

Gossip columns and gossip shows, water-cooler talks, tabloid newspapers, talk radio, internet social media – all can indeed turn a drop of "juicy info" into a raging social forest fire. In fact, there have been many cases where such pain has led to suicide. All because what is said in the context of a private, supporting conversation can be tragically misunderstood outside of the small group – especially by people that have not yet spit out the Apple. And remember, there is still an enemy lurking that would delight in destroying a group that is working to love God back.

Where is a good place for a small group to meet? It really depends on the background of the participants. My wife Debi and I have been part of a group of seven meeting for 4 years for breakfast at a local diner. I have been part of other groups that met for weekly lunches during work; evening dinner groups meeting monthly; prayer groups meeting weekly; and even an online group that communicated via chat room every 2 weeks. What you are looking for is a place of shared safety and comfort; a place where you can lean and share rather than recite and perform.

Small groups can grow and change; they can dissolve over time; they can split into two over time. Such is the nature of life. In my experience, such groups are places for love and holiness to grow, and for miracles to occur. After all, when it comes to loving God back, Christ said:

> *I also tell you this: If two of you agree here on earth concerning anything you ask, my Father in heaven will do it for you. For where two or three gather together as my followers, I am there among them. —Matthew 18:19–20 (NLT)*

So start a small group. Two is a small number; start there. Who do you ask? Why not sit and listen to God for a while, and see whose face pops into your head?

Discussion Questions

1. Close your eyes and see whose face appears. Write down their names. Do any of those names surprise you?

2. What makes it hard to keep a secret?

3. Have you ever been the object of a false rumor? Describe how it made you feel. Compare those feelings to how you feel when you repeat gossip.

Resilience vs. Fearfulness

Why do acts of evil seem to be stronger than acts of good on this earth?

I have a theory about this. Part of the reason is the magnifying power of evil, part of the reason is our reaction to evil, and part of the reason is our decision about who is in control of our lives.

Let's look at each of these three factors.

The Magnifying Power of Evil

Every single act of evil involves three groups: those who do evil, those who are harmed by evil, and those who witness the harm. Each of them are attacked by this single act in a different way – but each are attacked nonetheless.

Those who do an evil act are attacked by their own act! Each attack takes them further from a loving God. Each is committing a sin that adds to a debt that seems harder to forgive, making it harder for that person to believe they are redeemable. Each act may actually bring physical or emotional pleasure to those committing it, which increases the temptation to repeat the attack. Finally, each is adding to a growing debt of accountability that will be paid – either during this life, or when they face Christ for their final reckoning.

(What will that final reckoning look like? I personally am not sure. I pray that mercy and grace are still offered. I am certain God will be just. But most importantly, I work to spend every day loving God and man so much that I, personally, never have to doubt.)

Those who are directly harmed by the evil act endure pain and damage. Physical pain can include bleeding, organ injury, loss of function, and other damage that may or may not heal. Emotional damage may include immediate feelings of shock, betrayal, and anger; and the memory of the act can lead to the lingering recurrences of post-traumatic stress.

Those bystanders witnessing the evil act do not have to endure the physical damage, but their emotions are not so lucky. They can identify with the attacker, with all the emotional and spiritual repercussions the attacker suffers. They can identify with the victim, and feel all of the emotional and spiritual consequences the victim endures (filtered by each witness's preconceptions and past experiences).

The Reaction to Evil

The victim of evil can react in several damaging ways:

- "It's my fault. If I had stood up to them this wouldn't have happened." It is possible to learn from a mishap, but the victim has no control over the perpetrator of evil.

- "This is paying me back for being a bad person." The word *karma* does not appear in the Bible. If God was still in the retribution business, then Christ's sacrifice was meaningless.

- "If God loved me, He wouldn't ignore me." God is right there with you in this moment. He never ignores anyone.

- "God sent this person to punish me." God is love. God is never naughty.

- "If only I had stronger faith, this wouldn't have happened." Christ taught repeatedly that trials would occur in our lives. His life, with the world record for faith, was not trouble-free.

- "I'll pay you back for this." Repaying evil for evil never ends the cycle of pain; it only spreads it.

Onlookers can react in several damaging ways:

- "Is this going to happen to me next?" Panic and helplessness follow from giving power to the attacker over their lives.

- "God obviously won't fix this; I WILL!" Anger leads to vengeance – and more evil.

- "God must not be real if He let this happen." Suddenly, the pain of the act makes us believe we can fire God for not living up to our standards.

- "What's the use of trying if this will happen?" Suddenly, this close, intense memory pushes out all of the love and goodness we have ever experienced.

- "I don't need this in my life!" In an illusion of self-preservation, we build emotional distance and walls between us and the situation – even though those same walls keep out forgiveness and support.

All of this pain – all of this damage – from one act of evil. Imagine how only a few acts of evil can make all of us disbelieve all the good in creation?

The Decision of Sovereignty

The final factor in our reaction – the internal, almost subconscious factor – is our choice of who is in charge of us as we move forward from the act of evil. As we have said, there are three forces on the playing field of our individual Earthly existence. The first is God and his forces; the second is Satan and his forces; and the third – is our self.

In that brief, jaw-dropping moment – like the surprising finale of a magic trick – an evil act forces us to choose who is sovereign in our lives.

Is it the God of love – the one we have shown is real and next to you? The one who suddenly feels farther away? The one we have been distracted from in this moment?

Is it the enemy – who is fully equipped to manufacture new, more creative ways to tear us from our peace and joy? The enemy who wants to separate you from God and eradicate the idea of love?

Or is it your self – equipped with life, the power of free will, and with the Knowledge of Good and Evil, the Apple that Satan himself put in your hand?

We each vote for Sovereign – and we each decide how long it is until the next election.

Fortunately, there is a skill we can practice and perfect that guides us through this minefield.

Resilience versus Fearfulness

Resilience is defined as "the capacity to recover quickly from difficulties," and is a synonym of "toughness." It is a choice to look past difficulty and toward healing and perseverance.

Fearfulness is defined as "feeling afraid, showing fear or anxiety." It is a choice to look past current peace and safety and toward the next difficulty that will damage it.

Recent sociology and psychology research is looking at societal and cultural resilience. This means building systems of interaction that provide groups of people the support and resources to maintain and recover well-being. The opposite of a resilient culture is one with increasing layers of vigilance, suspicion, and enforcement to protect against the next problem.

The problem with fearfulness is that it devalues moments of joy and happiness. It assumes that perfect happiness is possible if we spend every waking moment exhausting ourselves working for it.

People who work to live uniformly happy lives without resilience will repeatedly be disappointed. We have built a fallen world. And every moment of disappointment is a request by the enemy to hold a new election for Sovereign.

Resilience, on the other hand, devalues moments of struggle and pain. Resilience accepts them as inevitable, to be sure; but the more resilient you are, the more you are able to look past it to the next moment of sweet relief; surprising joy; delightful victory.

Jesus was proof that a human life can be one of resilience. The disciples' behavior after Christ's death and resurrection showed that resilience can spread from persons, to small groups, to entire nations. Paul's life, illuminated in his letters, was a testimony to the superiority and victory of resilience in the face of trial.

Reacting to Evil in a Resilient Way

If you are the victim: first, mourn, pray for help, and reach to your support. Show your vulnerability; give yourself permission to show your hurt. Start the road to grieving. Remember, any grief includes denial, anger, depression, bargaining, and acceptance; experience those fully, but with your ever-present God, not by yourself.

Second, make it clear that what was done to you was NOT OK. If what happened to you was illegal, it is perfectly acceptable to seek legal justice – though not vengeance.

Third, work toward forgiving the person for their act. This has to be done to heal you; otherwise, the perpetrator of evil maintains control over you for life. This is NOT the same as excusing the act.

Remember, refusing your consent to be hurt is NOT judging the other person. It is a holy response that establishes you are NOT a willing victim, and that the action was hurtful. Also remember that law enforcement is accountable for the action, not judgment of the person. Each of us has broken the law at some point – the goal is not to condemn, but for the damager to "go and sin no more."

If you are the witness: first, mourn, pray for help, and reach out to give support. Think in terms of tangible assistance you can offer. Asking "how can I help?" to a shocked victim is not as helpful as "Who can I call for you?", "Do you want me to come over?", "Do you need help with chores or meals?", or "Can we pray together right now?".

Second, do not analyze the situation for "how you could have prevented it" or "if only this would have happened" or "I'll get that S.O.B. for you". Listen as the victim grieves (they are very likely to go through such phases), but your response is to listen, uplift, and support the victim.

Third, expect that you will go through your own grief. But before you share your pain with YOUR support, get permission from the victim, and tread very carefully. It is very easy for such ripples of support to turn into waves of gossip and uncontrolled emotion. It is OK to explain how you're feeling; but only rarely is it OK to share what the victim confidentially and personally shared. Those rare times include legal requirements to report abusive behavior to authorities – but again, inform the victim first.

Finally, if you are the damager: first, confess and repent. Now. Instantly. Not only to your victim, but to God, and to your support group.

Second, make it right to the best of your ability.

Third, if the victim is not ready to forgive, give them space and keep the door open for reconciliation. Remember that you cannot force the victim to go through that door.

Finally, ask God for forgiveness once again; learn how to make your repentance last; and forgive yourself. That does not mean forgetting the wrong; it means you are using it as a stop sign for your future behavior.

It is all about you. It is also about the person who last hurt you. It is also about the last victim you observed. It is also about All Of Us. Therefore, choosing yourself to be Sovereign ignores all of the rest, as well as the God who loves and created you. It is a choice for self-deception.

Choosing Satan to be Sovereign is a choice for fearfulness – because Satan wants you to be afraid, unloved and unlovable, and thus controlled. Evil acts are his currency.

Choosing God, Christ, and the Holy Spirit to be Sovereign is a choice for resilience – because God wants you to persevere, and feel love so fully that it flows out of you to everyone around you. Acts of love, grace, recovery, and forgiveness are His currency.

What do you want to practice?

Discussion Questions

1. What parts of your life do you have trouble giving up control over? What sins do you feel you are powerless to overcome?

2. Describe a personal tragedy that has made you stronger - and how.

3. Who in your life would help you improve at forgiving people?

The Ite People

In the late 1990's, a speaker came to our church with a special message for our youth. (It turned out to be a great message for us adults, too, but I digress.) This speaker, who wore a clown suit, began telling us a story called "Gideon Versus the Ite People". (For the original scripture, read Judges 3–8.)

She explained that in Gideon's time, the Israelites were living along with Canaanites, Hittites, Amorites, Perizzites, Hivites, Jebusites, Midianites, and Amelikites in the Promised land. God had made a covenant: if Israel would stay true to God's commandments (which included worshipping Him only), God would protect Israel. But he warned that if Israel violated their part of the covenant, things would not go well for them. And, of course, those Apple-chewing Israelites decided they knew as much as God, so they decided to worship made-up deities like Baal, Ashtoreth, Molech, and others.

However, some remained faithful to the covenant, so many times God would use one of those faithful to remind Israel of the truth of matters. Gideon was the example my clown friend chose for her story. She got tired of trying to pronounce all these nations, so she just decided to call them "the Ite people."

God commanded Gideon to attack the Ite people with an Army, and Gideon obeyed by amassing an army of 32,000. God realized that a victory by an army that large would be interpreted as human victory, so he ordered Gideon to reduce the army to 300 men – who then stood by and watched as their enemies turned on each other and routed themselves!

That would be a wonderful ending – except that within a generation, Israel was back to ignoring their covenant. And the Israelites were seen by the world as just another "Ite people" until King Saul came along – and again for generations between King Solomon and the arrival of Christ.

The New Ite People

Shortly after Christ's resurrection, as the apostles spread out to share the Holy Spirit, humans chewed their Apples and decided to make new kinds of Ite people – followers of a particular person's interpretation of the rules rather than a direct relationship to God through Christ. In the book of Acts, we read of disagreements between Paul, Peter, Silas, Barnabas, and others. In fact, Paul's first letter to the church in Corinth addressed this very phenomenon, and its destructive nature.

> *So look at Apollos and me as mere servants of Christ who have been put in charge of explaining God's mysteries. Now, a person who is put in charge as a manager must be faithful. As for me, it matters very little how I might be evaluated by you or by any human authority. I don't even trust my own judgment on this point. My conscience is clear, but that doesn't prove I'm right. It is the Lord Himself who will examine me and decide. –1 Corinthians 4:1–4 (NLT)*

Paul then spent a great deal of the rest of 1st Corinthians giving specific examples of behaviors that get in the way of loving God back. Unfortunately, most of us have turned those words into the New Mosaic Law to one degree or another – and have created entire new classes of Ite people.

Look at the United States of America today. Christ's message of unity, and of relationship with God at the center, has gone around the world several times over – but we are still Ite people.

Politically, we are Republicanites, Democratites, Progressivites, Leftites, Conservatites, Rightites, Libertarianites, Socialites, Capitalites, and lots of different flavors of Independites. And each group has various leaders, and each group has members who are more loyal to their tribe than they are to the Lord.

Even within the so-called Christian church, we have Baptistites, Methodites, Pentacostalites, Catholites, Episcopalites, Reformites, Lutherites, and thousands of others – all claiming that their set of rules is The Only Way to God.

What leads the Ite People

Small groups naturally combine to form large groups – that is part of how we function as human beings. But remember – those groups will take on the characteristic of their leading power. And as we have said, there are only three such powers: Humans, Satan, or God.

A group led by a person is only as good as the fallible human leader. The leader, if one arises, has two responsibilities: first, model loving God back, and second, correcting members of the group when they love the leader more than they love God. Because we are fallible, this can be incredibly hard to maintain – and when the love becomes focused on the human, it can go very wrong very fast.

A group led by Satan is one that focuses on a part of the world rather than the God who created it. Because Satan is so incredibly devious, many groups will not recognize that they have fallen. However, if the group starts saying things like "it is my God-given right to have (fill in the blank)," alarm bells should start to go off. Furthermore, if the group starts spreading gossip, disdain, or hatred toward someone NOT in the group, you can pretty much conclude that God is not in charge.

But watch it – what I have just said should NOT be used to decide a group's value. That is Apple-chewing in its most insidious form! Being aware of the possibilities should be used for only one purpose – to decide where YOU fit while practicing how to love God back. Can you express your concerns to your group members? Sure! That's part of the mutually supportive nature of groups. If the response is dialogue and contemplation, fantastic. But if the response is defensiveness and rebuke – you have a prayerful choice to make between God and the group. God may have you there to help Him reform the group. Then again, God may be leading you elsewhere.

Christ and the Ite People

Christ came to abolish the Ite people.

He deliberately chose the path of His ministry to include the excluded. The gospels are full of examples of how he loved and healed the excluded, the outsiders, and the undesirable. Keep in mind that, in John's Gospel, Christ revealed Himself as Messiah to a Samaritan woman very early in his ministry – look at the scripture once again:

> *"Sir," the woman said, "you must be a prophet. So tell me, why is it that you Jews insist that Jerusalem is the only place of worship, while we Samaritans claim it is here at Mount Gerizim, where our ancestors worshiped?" Jesus replied, "Believe me, dear woman, the time is coming when it will no longer matter whether you worship the Father on this mountain or in Jerusalem. You Samaritans know very little about the one you worship, while we Jews know all about him, for salvation comes through the Jews. But the time is coming—indeed it's here now—when true worshipers will worship the Father in spirit and in truth. The Father is looking for those who will worship him that way. For God is Spirit, so those who worship him must worship in spirit and in truth."*
>
> *The woman said, "I know the Messiah is coming—the one who is called Christ. When he comes, he will explain everything to us."*
>
> *Then Jesus told her, " I AM the Messiah!" – John 4:19–26 (NLT)*

When Jesus explained that the core of God's command for humankind was to love God back and love your neighbor as yourself, an Israelite asked for an example. Christ gave them one: a Samaritan.

> One day an expert in religious law stood up to test Jesus by asking him this question: "Teacher, what should I do to inherit eternal life?" Jesus replied, "What does the law of Moses say? How do you read it?" The man answered, "'You must love the Lord your God with all your heart, all your soul, all your strength, and all your mind.' And, 'Love your neighbor as yourself.'" "Right!" Jesus told him. "Do this and you will live!" The man wanted to justify his actions, so he asked Jesus, "And who is my neighbor?"

> Jesus replied with a story: "A Jewish man was traveling from Jerusalem down to Jericho, and he was attacked by bandits. They stripped him of his clothes, beat him up, and left him half dead beside the road.

> "By chance a priest came along. But when he saw the man lying there, he crossed to the other side of the road and passed him by. A Temple assistant walked over and looked at him lying there, but he also passed by on the other side.

"Then a despised Samaritan came along, and when he saw the man, he felt compassion for him. Going over to him, the Samaritan soothed his wounds with olive oil and wine and bandaged them. Then he put the man on his own donkey and took him to an inn, where he took care of him. The next day he handed the innkeeper two silver coins, telling him, 'Take care of this man. If his bill runs higher than this, I'll pay you the next time I'm here.'

"Now which of these three would you say was a neighbor to the man who was attacked by bandits?" Jesus asked. The man replied, "The one who showed him mercy." Then Jesus said, "Yes, now go and do the same." –Luke 10:25–37 (NLT)

This was NOT what the Israelite wanted to hear. But it was the truth.

Christ came to abolish the Ite people.

Stop Being an Ite People

In order to stop being one of the Ite people; in order to remain part of a God-centered group; in order to be part of this world's solution rather than part of the problem – you have to follow two simple paths. We just heard them.

You must love the Lord your God with all your heart, all your soul, all your strength, and all your mind.

You must love your neighbor as yourself.

And every member of every group is your neighbor.

So you must love them all with all of God's love.

Nothing about "Discerning Good and Evil" is mentioned in these paths.

Discussion Questions

1. What group do you feel treats you like an inferior? Describe how you feel about that group. What do you have in common with that group?

2. What groups do you identify with? What do you feel you gain by being part of this group?

3. What negative words do people use to describe Christians? What steps can you take to change those opinions?

We are All Headed to Golgotha

You know, in all of this discussion of good and evil, Satan and God, love and power – I have only made a passing reference to one of the pivotal concepts in this world.

Death.

Everything with DNA on this planet – dies.

By death, I mean every organism's physical processes stop. The organism decays and becomes food for some other organism, be it a predator or a bacterium. We never see that organism on this planet again.

Death is the worst separation we can experience – and one of Satan's most nasty advertising tools.

Death is painful

For most of us, nearly all of our memory, experience, and relationships are with other people on this Earth.

Death ends all Earthly relationships.

Ends.

For the deceased, and for all those who have a relationship with the deceased, Ending can feel like failure; loss of control; a personal loss of a part of their heart and soul; or all three.

This is never fun. Even in situations where end of life is inevitable, and prepared for (such as through hospice services for the terminally ill), death is still incredibly painful.

For me, I had 10 weeks between the start of hospice care for Terri, and the 18 hours of watching her die. She lay unconscious and gasping in our bed until her heart finally stopped. Thanks to the hospice care, I was certain Terri wasn't suffering. But eight years later, I still weep as I type this.

For my Godgift Debi, the pain was similar. Her first husband, Mike, was diagnosed with untreatable prostate cancer 2 1/2 years before his death. They had hospice help with pain relief the last 4 days before his surprising death. The two of us, and her sons, still mourn fourteen years later.

Death is separation

I am certain that Mike and Terri are smiling and joyful in God's embrace. I have no idea what that looks like, even though scripture has plenty of poetic suggestions. But except for rare glimpses like the rainbow story I shared in the beginning of this book, Debi and I are completely unable to communicate with Mike and Terri.

That hurts. A lot.

Most grief counselors will tell you: you don't get over that kind of grief. You get used to it. Grief, or necessity, builds resilience in order for the griever to survive and live on. But we cannot – we should not – forget that the love ever existed. The love of others is part of what creates us, and we must incorporate that love, plus the separation, into a new "normal".

There have been thousands of people who have claimed to have the psychic ability to speak with the dead. Scripture warns us against approaching such people, and I believe there are two reasons why. First, the vast majority have been proven to be deceivers using tricks and manipulation to deceive us.[26] Second, there is the hypothesis that demonic forces could mimic departed loved ones for the sake of causing great harm. In my personal practice of loving God back, I choose God's advice over these two risks that show no

---

[26] I encourage you to read the writings of James Randi, world-famous magician and skeptic, on this subject. Although Randi is a self-described atheist, his description of his beliefs could be described as agnostic, because he takes the existence or absence of God as unprovable. Therefore, Randi chooses not to seek an answer to that question.

benefit. Debi and I will be reunited with Mike and Terri eventually. But for now, it still hurts Debi and I.

Death has been conquered

Until Christ, the concept of eternal life with God was foreign. In the old testament, there is precious little evidence of people who escape earthly death and ascend into heaven. Enoch was specifically singled out in the lineage from Adam to Noah recounted in Genesis 5; verse 24 states that at age 365, "he disappeared, because God took him." All of the others mentioned in that chapter died. In 2 Kings 2:12, Elisha watched his mentor Elijah as he was carried on a chariot of fire to heaven.

However, in Luke 9:28–36, Jesus is shown having a dazzling conference with Moses and Elijah! This meeting, witnessed by disciples Peter, James and John, was considered so important that it is also mentioned in Mark 9:2–9 and Matthew 17:1–8. How could this happen, since Moses died (according to Deuteronomy 34:1–6)? God certainly had a special relationship with Moses, since scripture states that they had many face-to-face conversations. We don't know; but clearly, Moses lived on. This demonstrates that God, creator of the universe, had the intent for people to continue living after an earthly death.

It is when God comes to earth in the form of Jesus that this power is completely made manifest. Even after whipping, the agonizing torture of crucifixion, a spear wound in the liver, and burial in a sealed tomb guarded by Roman soldiers to prevent grave robbers – Christ appeared many times on this earth. And before and after His resurrection, Jesus offered the same to us.

Death is a lie

Therefore, death is a lie. If Christ is real, then life after earthly death is real. And to someone who believes in God and Christ, fear of death is simply another fear of another lie. As my darling Terri said to many friends in her last month on this planet: "I'm very sad – but I'm not scared."

How could I not work every day to love back a God who had personally accomplished that for me?

Death is a motivator

Now as I type this, I am 63 years old. Debi and I are extremely conscious of our stage of life, and we thank God every morning that we get to spend together. But we are attending the funerals of more and more friends and neighbors, and we cannot predict when it will be our turn.

I do not fear earthly death. But I am on the way to my Golgotha.

That reality drives me to cram three things into every single day I have left. I will love God back with all that I am. I will love and bless others with all that I am. And I will take every opportunity to show others the loving, grace-filled, forgiving, intentional way to Christ.

Which means striving every day to spit out the Apple.

Discussion Questions

1. Do you have a bucket list? How would it change if you had one year to live? If you had one month to live?

2. List up to 5 people who would mourn your death. What do they know about your faith?

3. Do you know someone who died an atheist? Describe how that made you feel.

Scorecards are Apple-flavored

How am I doing?

That question haunts me, even after years of Christ telling me I can stop worrying about it.

I asked it of Terri, every few weeks. I used to ask it of Debi, every few weeks. I asked it of every military supervisor I worked for, like clockwork, every 90 days. I ask it of my accountability brothers when I'm feeling down. And I ask it of God – every single morning.

When I started asking this, it was out of fear of failing. Through unfortunate circumstances, I learned from my parents that I was only a worthwhile human being if I worked my butt off. Whenever I slacked off, my worthiness plummeted in a hurry. I'm not sure if that was the lesson they wanted to teach, but that was what I learned.

When I discovered I was pretty smart, and pretty good in school, I learned another lesson. If I kept score of my accomplishments, and racked up a string of A's and 100's on my schoolwork, I could easily become a very smart person who was conceited and insufferable to everyone around me.

Finally, though, around 10th grade, I started to learn that if I shared my blessings with others, and worked to care for them while caring for myself, I could still grow while developing a growing network of meaningful, positive relationships.

Much later, I learned that was what God had in mind in the first place.

How are you doing?

Some of you reading this book may be looking for a scorecard. A checklist. A quiz that you can score to determine your quality as a Christian or effectiveness as a disciple.

I hate to break it to you. I have no idea what such a quiz would look like. And I wouldn't want to guess.

Why?

Because scorecards are Apple-flavored.

As we have discussed all through this book, judging your worth as a human being is something God expressly warned us against doing when He told us to stay away from the Apple. It is something Satan worked hard to make us do when he showed us the Apple. And it is something we are exquisitely practiced at doing since we have eaten the Apple.

This system of self-judging is very common. We live with human evaluation tools from kindergarten on up. We call them tests, quizzes, evaluation tools, and performance reviews. But the thing we forget to teach is that these are measures of behavior and skills. These are measures of human *doings*, not human *beings*.

How does God think you are doing?

If you ask God how you are as a human being, He will answer "you are my own dear child, and I love you."

If you ask God how you are doing at being holy, He will answer "not good enough to be holy to enter Heaven on your own."

We know this because scripture has examples of people asking that very question.

The book of Matthew tells of a wealthy young man who came to Jesus looking for a report card:

> *Someone came to Jesus with this question: "Teacher, what good deed must I do to have eternal life?"*
>
> *"Why ask me about what is good?" Jesus replied. "There is only One who is good. But to*

answer your question—if you want to receive eternal life, keep the commandments."

"Which ones?" the man asked. And Jesus replied: "'You must not murder. You must not commit adultery. You must not steal. You must not testify falsely. Honor your father and mother. Love your neighbor as yourself.' "

"I've obeyed all these commandments," the young man replied. "What else must I do?"

Jesus told him, "If you want to be perfect, go and sell all your possessions and give the money to the poor, and you will have treasure in heaven. Then come, follow me."

But when the young man heard this, he went away sad, for he had many possessions.

Then Jesus said to his disciples, "I tell you the truth, it is very hard for a rich person to enter the Kingdom of Heaven. I'll say it again—it is easier for a camel to go through the eye of a needle than for a rich person to enter the Kingdom of God!"

The disciples were astounded. "Then who in the world can be saved?" they asked.

Jesus looked at them intently and said, "Humanly speaking, it is impossible. But with

God everything is possible."–Matthew 19:16–26 (NLT)

The Pharisee Nicodemus had the same question in mind when he tried to secretly meet with Jesus one evening. Jesus answered his question even before Nicodemus could ask it:

> There was a man named Nicodemus, a Jewish religious leader who was a Pharisee. After dark one evening, he came to speak with Jesus. "Rabbi," he said, "we all know that God has sent you to teach us. Your miraculous signs are evidence that God is with you."
>
> Jesus replied, "I tell you the truth, unless you are born again, you cannot see the Kingdom of God."
>
> "What do you mean?" exclaimed Nicodemus. "How can an old man go back into his mother's womb and be born again?"
>
> Jesus replied, "I assure you, no one can enter the Kingdom of God without being born of water and the Spirit. Humans can reproduce only human life, but the Holy Spirit gives birth to spiritual life. So don't be surprised when I say, 'You must be born again.' The wind blows wherever it wants. Just as you can hear the wind

but can't tell where it comes from or where it is
going, so you can't explain how people are born
of the Spirit."

"How are these things possible?" Nicodemus
asked.

Jesus replied, "You are a respected Jewish
teacher, and yet you don't understand these
things? I assure you, we tell you what we know
and have seen, and yet you won't believe our
testimony. But if you don't believe me when I tell
you about earthly things, how can you possibly
believe if I tell you about heavenly things? No
one has ever gone to heaven and returned. But
the Son of Man has come down from heaven.
And as Moses lifted up the bronze snake on a
pole in the wilderness, so the Son of Man must
be lifted up, so that everyone who believes in
him will have eternal life.

"For this is how God loved the world: He
gave his one and only Son, so that everyone who
believes in him will not perish but have eternal
life. God sent his Son into the world not to judge
the world, but to save the world through him.
There is no judgment against anyone who
believes in him. But anyone who does not believe
in him has already been judged for not believing
in God's one and only Son. And the judgment is

based on this fact: God's light came into the world, but people loved the darkness more than the light, for their actions were evil. All who do evil hate the light and refuse to go near it for fear their sins will be exposed. But those who do what is right come to the light so others can see that they are doing what God wants." –John 3:1–21 (NLT)

This passage shows that our behavior does matter – but if we focus on our own behavior, we are doomed. Jesus acknowledged when people got close:

One of the teachers of religious law was standing there listening to the debate. He realized that Jesus had answered well, so he asked, "Of all the commandments, which is the most important?"

Jesus replied, "The most important commandment is this: 'Listen, O Israel! The LORD our God is the one and only LORD. And you must love the LORD your God with all your heart, all your soul, all your mind, and all your strength.' The second is equally important: 'Love your neighbor as yourself.' No other commandment is greater than these."

The teacher of religious law replied, "Well said, Teacher. You have spoken the truth by

*saying that there is only one God and no other.
And I know it is important to love him with all
my heart and all my understanding and all my
strength, and to love my neighbor as myself. This
is more important than to offer all of the burnt
offerings and sacrifices required in the law."*

*Realizing how much the man understood,
Jesus said to him, "You are not far from the
Kingdom of God." And after that, no one dared
to ask him any more questions. —Mark 12:28–34
(NLT)*

Even here, though, Jesus did not say, "You
are good enough," or "you are holy enough."
He described the teacher as "not far from the
Kingdom."

Paul, in Romans 3:20, says, "For no one can
ever be made right with God by doing what
the law commands." He re-emphasizes this in
verse 23: "For everyone has sinned; we all fall
short of God's glorious standards."

What is God doing about it?

He already did the most important thing.

He came down as Jesus and demonstrated
that God cares more about loving us than He
does about punishing us. Not only that, He
cares more about loving *every single human*

being, not only the people of Israel. God will indeed keep His promises to Israel, but not because they are more holy than anyone else. God will keep His promises because God keeps promises.

But that doesn't mean that God is sitting back and waiting for us to re-take the holiness exam. God is pursuing us even today. That pursuit takes the form of telling those who love Him to get good at loving everyone. It all comes back to turning off evaluation and turning on cherishing.

What are YOU doing about it?

See how different that question is? Compare it to, "How am I doing?" Asking how you are doing is asking for a label; a score; a judgment; a *noun*.

Christ died to make those nouns irrelevant. He endured torturous punishment for you before you sinned enough to require it. You are pursued, loved, valued, redeemed. Those words are *verbs*.

What verbs will you use? What actions will you take? Look at the Great Commandment again:

> *Jesus replied, "The most important commandment is this: 'Listen, O Israel! The*

LORD our God is the one and only LORD. And you must love the LORD your God with all your heart, all your soul, all your mind, and all your strength.' The second is equally important: 'Love your neighbor as yourself.' No other commandment is greater than these. —Mark 12:29–31 (NLT)

There are only two verbs in that quote.

The first one, "is," is a form of "I AM."

The second is "love."

What am I doing about it?

I am trying, though sometimes failing, to love. I think I'm getting better at it with practice.

Instead of asking Debi: "Am I a good enough husband?", I ask: "Do you feel loved enough?" (Verb, not noun.)

When I meet with my support group, I share both my delights and struggles, and I work to listen to theirs.

I spend the first part of my day talking to God and listening to Him.

I read the Bible and two devotionals each morning.

I look for opportunities to thank God all through every day.

I try to bless everyone I come in contact with.

When I hear someone labelling or berating themselves, I find my first opportunity to compliment some action they have taken, and make a point of reminding them that they are loved by God, and by me.

When I hear someone berating a third party, if I am asked, I try to look for a perspective that avoids condemnation. I focus on helping the speaker mourn and heal from their injury. And I look for paths to reconciliation. Unfortunately, sometimes I don't see any such paths, in which case my response stops at empathy and sympathy.

I speak up for love and justice whenever I have the opportunity.

Oh, yeah – and I listen to my wife when she advises me to write a book.

Is this the magic formula? Nope. It's not good enough to earn me a ticket to Heaven. I'm no better a person than you are. I'm still a sinner.

It's all just thanking Christ constantly for buying that ticket with His life.

It's all just loving Him back.

Discussion Questions

1. What activities help you feel closer to God?

2. Describe a time when your performance on a task disappointed you. Who helped you deal with it?

3. Close your eyes and think of three people who do not feel loved enough. How could you love them?

Here! Have a present! I love you!

I am either real, evil, insane, or mythical. My wife, sons and friends can testify to my reality, so that rules out mythical. My legal and military history is clean except for a couple of traffic stupidities as a youth, so I'm confident that rules out evil. My family doctor, Dave Schriemer, assures me I am not insane.

You are real and not mythical. I don't care about whether you are evil or insane. I love you, God loves you, and there isn't anything you can do about it.

Christ is either real, evil, insane, or mythical. I believe He is real. I hope I have loved you enough to give you a path to accept Him as real.

You have the free will to decide about Christ – but regardless, Christ has blessed me with the opportunity to give you this love present. He has also blessed you with the present of Love, and the astounding, forgiving present called Grace.

Max Lucado once said, "To accept grace is to accept the vow to share grace."

Wouldn't you rather enjoy these presents – instead of trying to enjoy a nasty piece of well-chewed Apple?

God Bless.

P.S. I am thankful for Willem Renzema, one of the first readers of this book, for painstakingly logging the typos that I and seven proofreaders missed.

————

I would welcome your considered feedback in the form of a review on Amazon for this book. Not as a scorecard; scorecards are Apple-flavored. Amazon feedback in the form of an honest review is the best way you can help put this book in the hands of others who need it.

Made in the USA
Coppell, TX
16 February 2023